Spectacular World of

Southern African
Birds

Reader's Digest

Spectacular World of Southern African Birds

In association with
Mercedes-Benz of South Africa

Published by The Reader's Digest Association South Africa (Pty) Limited, Cape Town

Consultant:
Professor Phil Hockey, BSc (Hons), PhD
University of Cape Town

Editor: Rod Baker
Art Editor: Christabel Hardacre
Researcher/Writer: Taryn James
Cartographer: Augusta Prohn
Project co-ordinator: Grant Moore
Indexer: Sarah Maddox

Spectacular World of Southern African Birds
was edited and designed by
The Reader's Digest Association South Africa (Pty) Limited,
130 Strand Street, Cape Town 8001.

ISBN 1-874912-83-1

*Gregarious Cattle Egrets, their wings a pale blur in the dawn's weak
light, take to the air from a reed bed where they roosted overnight.*

PAGE 1: *A Barred Owl*

FACING TITLE PAGE: *A group of Ostriches*

Every now and then an African Jacana will stop its dainty walk across an expanse of water lilies in search of food and lift the edge of a water-lily leaf, hoping to find a mollusc, crustacean or insect beneath.

Our wonderful heritage

Nature has endowed southern Africa with bountiful wildlife, not least of which are the many bird species to be found on the subcontinent. Some are permanent residents, others are unique to this region, and some visit us from as far afield as the Arctic to breed here.

However, people accustomed to splendour often tend to appreciate it less than others seeing it for the first time, 'After fifteen minutes nobody looks at a rainbow', wrote the poet and naturalist Johann Wolfgang von Goethe, and it would be a sad day for the people of this region should they ever reach the stage where they no longer cherish birds as vital to the natural heritage of future generations.

Mercedes-Benz is proud to be associated with this magnificent volume. I trust the book will awaken greater awareness of the wealth of southern African bird life, give new enjoyment to readers already familiar with it, and accentuate the importance of protecting and conserving its spectacular variety.

Christoph Köpke
Chairman
Mercedes-Benz of South Africa

A Red Bishop, resplendent in its breeding plumage, displays from a perch to attract females to the nests it has built.

Contents

Rock Pigeons, commonly seen throughout southern Africa, can nest almost anywhere.

The distribution of birds in southern Africa depends largely on the physical nature of a particular environment. Orangebreasted Sunbirds, for example, are at home only in fynbos whereas Yellow Canaries thrive in fynbos, as well as in a variety of other regions. For this reason, the book is organized by natural regions – as shown on the map opposite and the contents list on this page.

Supplementing the regional sections are special features covering certain aspects of bird behaviour.

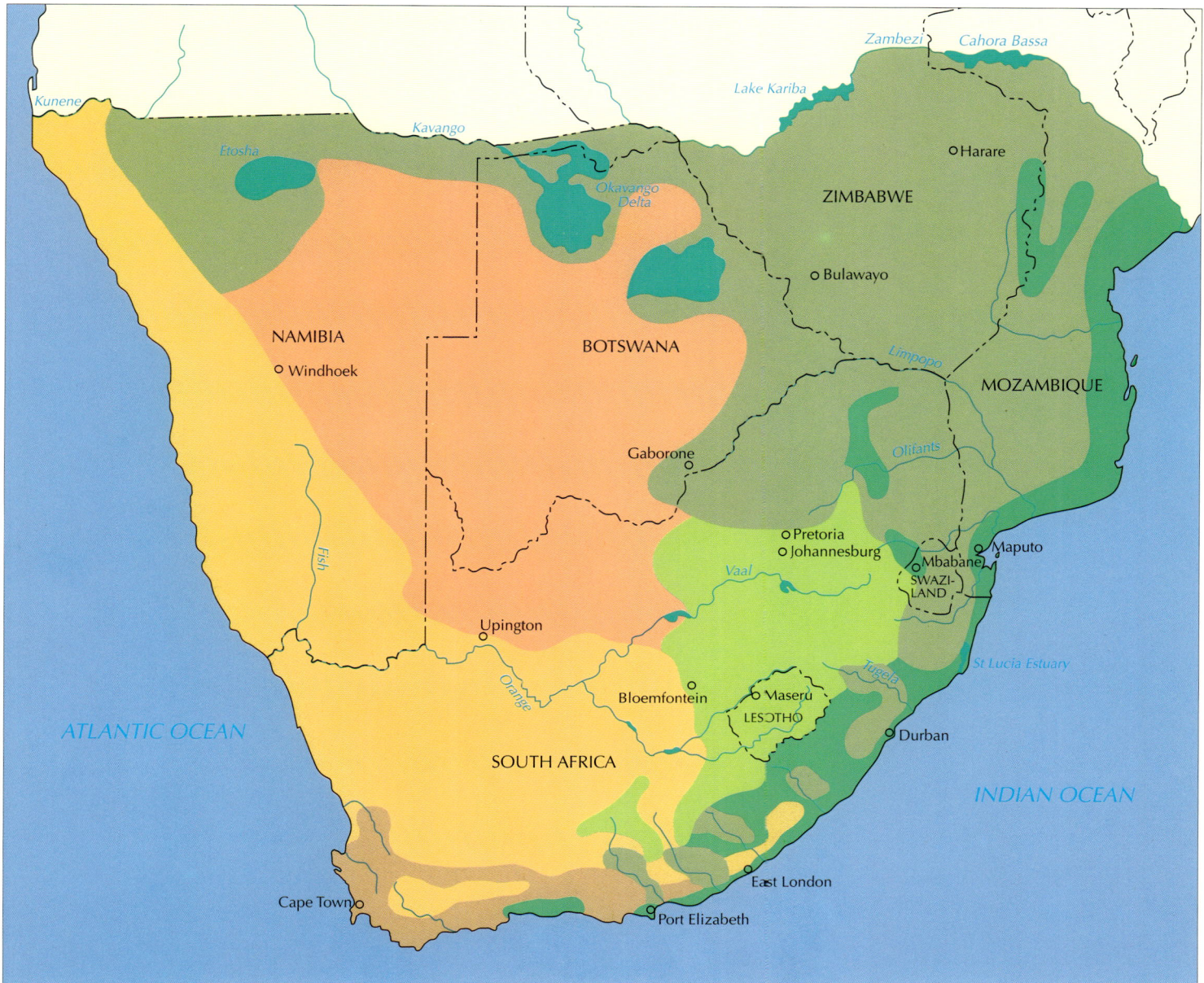

THE NATURAL REGIONS OF SOUTHERN AFRICA

Each of these regions, and the birds found there, represents a chapter in the book – as indicated by the page numbers below.

Map labels:

ATLANTIC OCEAN
INDIAN OCEAN

NAMIBIA
BOTSWANA
ZIMBABWE
MOZAMBIQUE
SOUTH AFRICA
LESOTHO
SWAZI-LAND

Windhoek
Gaborone
Harare
Bulawayo
Pretoria
Johannesburg
Maseru
Bloemfontein
Upington
Durban
East London
Port Elizabeth
Cape Town
Mbabane
Maputo

Kunene
Kavango
Etosha
Okavango Delta
Lake Kariba
Zambezi
Cahora Bassa
Limpopo
Olifants
Fish
Orange
Vaal
Tugela
St Lucia Estuary

Legend:

- Fynbos *10*
- Arid savannah *132*
- Forests *24*
- Deserts and semi-deserts *164*
- Grasslands and mountains *54*
- Wetlands *186*
- Eastern woodlands *84*
- Marine *228*

Where the Sugarbird sips from flowers born of fire

Dusty mauves and silvery greens, muted in misty winter rains, colour the fynbos that clothes the southwestern tip of Africa, unsurpassed in its beauty and variety. This delicately balanced and diverse shrubland is patchworked into the greater Cape floral kingdom, covering the rugged mountains of the most southern and western parts of the Cape and stretching across its valleys and coastal plains with a breathtaking range of visual intensity. Unique to southern Africa, fynbos, or macchia, is a richly hued and textured tapestry woven from the threads of more than 7 000 plant species.

More than half of these are exceedingly rare. Some are teetering on the edge of extinction, restricted to small, specific habitats, like the snow protea that grows only above the snow line in the Cederberg.

Rooting tenaciously in mineral-poor soil and designed to defy wet winters, hot dry summers and pitiless winds, fynbos, or 'fine bush', is characterized by the heathlike erica that flourishes in splendid clusters of colour; tall, big-flowered proteas with broad leathery leaves; spiky reedlike restioids and the world's most beautiful bulbous plants. Despite its extraordinary botanical diversity, there is a strange poverty of bird species in this region as the food supply is in fact meagre and unvaried. Nevertheless, this austere and inhospitable habitat is the only home of the Victorin's Warbler, Cape Siskin, Protea Canary, Cape Sugarbird, Cape Rockjumper and Orangebreasted Sunbird.

The last, a nectar drinker, depends on the vivid erica species for nourishment and, like the sugarbird, is a valuable pollinator as it flits from flower to flower. It furiously defends a favoured feeding site – its metallic green head cocked above its orange waistcoat clashing wonderfully with the vibrant crimsons and vermilions of the Cape heaths.

Noisy and conspicuous above a voluptuous display of flowering proteas, a Cape Sugarbird swoops and dances in an elaborate aerial courtship for the watching female – its long tail tracing loops and curves in the air with a stylish flourish. Endemic to southern Africa, this nectar-drinking bird is found only in those parts of the Cape fynbos where proteas abound and it has developed a

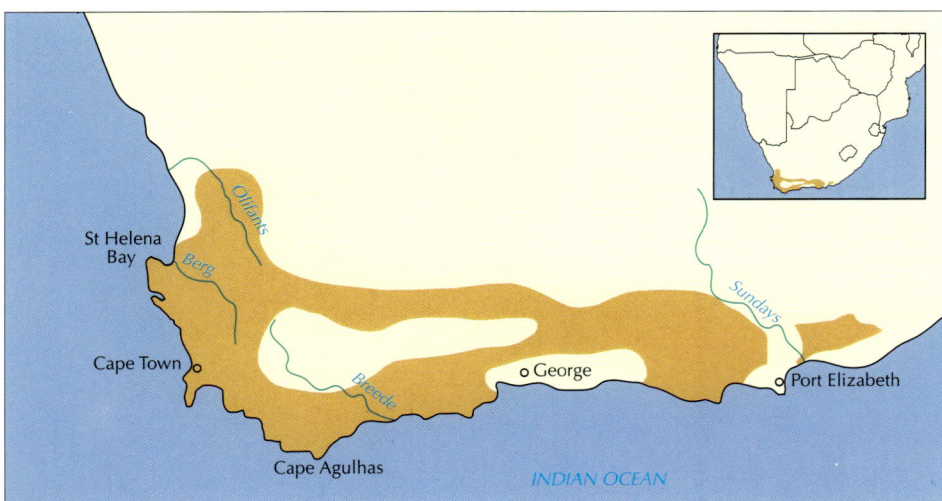

FYNBOS

The Cape Sugarbird, closely associated with proteas, breeds and nests in the wetter winter months when the proteas are in flower and there is less threat from fire.

fierce and loyal partnership with these plants. It may sip nectar from the flower with its long curved bill, perch on the highest spray to snap at a passing insect or use the bush as a nest site. The female lays her eggs in a nest built in the lee of a thick-leaved protea bush where it will be most protected from the howling Cape winds and relentless winter rains.

To further protect the young, the cup of the nest is tenderly lined with down that the bird has plucked from the heart of the protea. In return for succour and shelter, the sugarbird obligingly transfers pollen from bush to bush as it visits each one to probe and feed.

The intricate relationship that exists between bird and plant, and the remarkable range of natural settings in the Cape – from the Cape Peninsula's sheer sandstone and granite cliffs, looming up from treacherous seas, to serene

Hunters delight in the Greywing Francolin's habit of crouching in the undergrowth and suddenly bursting into flight when disturbed.

Elevated importantly on a spiky termite mound, this male Southern Black Korhaan boldly and raucously calls out across the fynbos. The sound can be heard from a kilometre away and is assumed to be an attempt to attract the quieter, more secretive female into its territory.

and fragrant valleys framed by undulating hills – bring a heady and sensual quality to birding in the fynbos.

In the rugged Swartland you may be surprised by a Cape Francolin as it suddenly scuttles out of the bushes and explodes into flight under the watchful eyes of a Jackal Buzzard circling darkly in the sky overhead. Here, where the air is filled with the sweet scent of buchu, you may also see a Greybacked Cisticola, light and anxious as it darts from bush to grass tuft. The sound of its loud call, a strangely musical *prrreee teee teee,* rings high in your ears.

Then there are the secret places, where rock pools the colour of weak black tea are harboured in deep gorges and fed by cascades of the purest water. Here, in the dappled shadows, a Victorin's Warbler may hide. Lilting and sibilant, its song spills out over the dense vegetation in which it forages. It flies with its tail spread and flicks it up and down agitatedly when perched on a bush or rock. More likely to be heard than seen, a glimpse of this shy bird is a rare treat.

In a world that the Xhosa describe as where, 'the wonderful and the impossible have come into collision', the most extraordinary element in the evolution of fynbos is fire. Awesome and feared, fire, for all its destructiveness, is the life force of many fynbos plants as its heat stimulates germination of seeds lying dormant in the soil or held fast in the flowerheads of some proteas.

The more opportunistic birds feed on the insects that have been flushed out on the edge of the advancing fire, while the Cape Siskin picks its way through the smoking black moonscape, foraging for seeds that have burst from cones. But generally, birds of the fynbos shrewdly avoid the threat of ravenous fire by confining their breeding and nesting to the wetter winter months.

Although the fragile ecosystem of the fynbos is acknowledged as a world treasure, it is surrendering slowly to the creeping violation of urbanization, agricultural encroachment and man-made fires – its bird numbers dwindling along with their precious habitat.

Fynbos has become a national treasure under siege.

The Steppe Buzzard, a Eurasian migrant, escapes northern winters to enjoy the Cape summer. It drops from a perch onto its prey.

A Blackshouldered Kite wags its tail vigorously up and down conspicuously. After feeding it may rest for a few hours before hunger drives it to hunt again. It does so from perches and also by hovering and then plunging onto prey with wings stretched high above its back.

LIKE A BOLT FROM THE BLUE

The Blackshouldered Kite, one of the smaller, less menacing raptors, is often seen perched on the highest branch of a tree or on a telephone pole. It is an accomplished hunter: at the slightest movement in the grass it drops towards its unsuspecting victim, legs outstretched, and snatches it up with its talons. It usually preys on small rodents.

Sometimes, however, it flies into the breeze, flapping its wings in a circular motion to hover in one spot while it scans the ground for prey. This is true hovering, its superb coordination ensuring that the bird's head remains still, so that its vision remains crisp and unblurred.

These birds hunt alone or in pairs by day, but at night they share untidy communal roosts in reed beds or high trees with up to 300 individuals.

Keen sight and the ability to judge distances are vital for hunting. Thus raptors, such as this Blackshouldered Kite, have eyes set at the front of the head, enabling objects to be seen three-dimensionally. This juvenile (like the one opposite) will have bright red eyes when an adult.

A fledgling Orangebreasted Sunbird feeds from the trumpet-like flower of an Erica patersonia. It uses its long tubular tongue, which is split at the end for drinking nectar, to take sustenance from the depths of the bloom.

One of the most stunningly coloured sunbirds, the male Orangebreasted Sunbird, defends its territory aggressively, posturing wildly to ward off any of its fellow sunbirds that dare to approach its food supply. It enjoys bathing in the dew on wide protea leaves.

Firmly grasping a freshly snapped insect, a Grassbird settles on a protea before eating its meal. Its name comes from its unusual habit of preferring to skulk in the undergrowth rather than fly away when disturbed.

The Cape Sugarbird eats nectar and insects – taken in flight or from its perch on a flower. Other birds shelter from strong winds but this bird's sharp claws enable it to grip tightly onto a protea and continue drinking and pollinating. This female's tail is shorter than the male's.

Stirring the murky water with persuasive feet, the Yellowbilled Stork forages with easy patience. Its partially open bill will snap shut on any creature that brushes against it. Sometimes one wing will be gracefully extended to lure small fish into its shadow.

From the serene and solitary fishing of herons to the majestic communal feeding of pelicans, fish-eating birds have many intriguing ways of hunting and capturing their slippery prey.

The Grey Heron stalks its quarry with elegant stealth and snatches it from the water with one quick stretch of its long neck. Pelicans co-operate in fishing parties, herding fish into the shallows to be scooped up in their pouched beaks and African Skimmers glide across still waters, their lower mandibles just slicing the surface. The moment one touches a fish, the beak snaps shut and the wriggling morsel is swallowed.

Less subtle is the Cape Gannet which simply dive-bombs its prey from a spectacular height and snatches a fish on the way back up to the surface.

The Black Egret will hold this pose for about 3 seconds at a time, quickly jabbing at fish that have darted into the shade of the canopy formed by its wings.

The Redbilled Teal, a common sight on southern African waters, fishes in a peculiar but effective way. Feeding mainly in the morning or late evening, it floats awhile and then suddenly upends itself for a quick underwater reconnaissance – and, it hopes, a catch.

With startling speed and deadly accuracy, this Grey Heron strikes at its prey – unfooled by the distorted view that refraction of the water creates.

A lone grey fisherman, catch firmly gripped with no chance of wriggling free, saunters casually through the cool waters in no apparent hurry to gulp down his meal. A quietly alert feeder, the Grey Heron eats almost anything it encounters, including small birds and reptiles.

This protesting fish is about to be flipped, so that it can be swallowed by the Grey Heron headfirst, with the scales and spine folded flat. The technique is used by most fishing birds, notably Darters – which toss fish high into the air before swallowing them.

Secret dwellers that haunt the deep forests

In a land that is essentially dry and rain-neglected, it is not surprising that the forests of southern Africa occupy a relatively small area. The three types – patches of lowland forest on the northern and central coasts of KwaZulu-Natal, the narrow band of coastal forest from there to just west of Port Elizabeth, and Afromontane forests that extend from the Tsitsikamma in the south to the eastern escarpment of the Northern Province – are individually and collectively home to a rich variety of bird species.

The arboreal jewel of the southern Cape is the dark and ancient Tsitsikamma, a forest of indigenous trees that flourish in kloofs, valleys and river gorges. The light falls softly in this beautiful Eden, filtered through a thick canopy of leaves and knotted branches held aloft by tall, handsome yellowwoods, ironwoods and red alders, sturdy giants above feathery tree ferns and disordered heaps of twisted roots.

The hushed depths, where the sun barely penetrates the dense foliage, are quieter than the busier fringe where the air resounds with the rowdy chorus of birds and cicadas.

Further east, in the coastal forest, the owls begin to stir as dusk nears, blinking in the thin twilight. The slight movement they make as they shift position provokes a sudden explosion of fluttering wings and indignant screeching as a cloud of drongos and robins mob the night birds. The Squaretailed Drongo, a noisy, thieving bird, is intensely aggressive and bold in the defence of its nest – a neat cup of lichens and plants bound with spiders' webs and slung hammock-like in the fork of a tree. It fearlessly attacks larger raptors, including the Crowned Eagle, monarch of the forest, insistently dive-bombing and pecking at the raptor until it flees its territory. Satisfied, the drongo resumes its own restless hawking. It snaps at insects that flick by its perch on the edge of a small clearing in the wood or bullies smaller birds into releasing their catches.

The banished eagle flies to an area where, unharassed, it will be able to hunt by dropping onto an animal from the lower limbs of a large tree. Like other forest raptors, it is able to manoeuvre through the tight confines of this habitat with extraordinary agility.

Most birds in the deep, tangled heart of the forests are less conspicuous and lead intensely covert lives, relying on loud calls to communicate with one another. The mournful cry of the tiny Buffspotted Flufftail, which rises hauntingly from the wetter coastal forests, resembles the sound of a very distant train, and is often said to be the howl of a departed soul. This bird is so rarely detected that its eerie call has sometimes been attributed instead to a lizard, a chameleon or even a puff adder. At times a flufftail may hum or even

FORESTS

A croaking purr draws attention to the little-known African Barred Owl perched on a high bough.

growl – a ghostly sound when the source is concealed in a darkly shadowed grove of trees on a mist-shrouded night.

This elusive bird spends much of its time on the ground, scuttling rodent-like through the undergrowth, its chicks following closely as they forage and scratch for insects, snails and small seeds. Their nest is a rough dome of ferns and leaves on the forest floor.

Birdspotting in indigenous forests can be enormously frustrating as birds are well hidden and often further aided in their concealment by skilful camouflage. From their secret perches, they are able to see you before you get a chance to see them. The challenge then is to be alert to the many clues and hints left by these forest dwellers.

A single feather dotted with white spots, each distinctly circled in neon blue, reveals that a Crested Guineafowl recently passed that way. An untidy littering of droppings on the ground may mark the site of an owl's roosting place.

In the valley bushveld of the Eastern Cape, where *Euphorbia* trees are abundant, extreme patience may be rewarded by a rare glimpse of the exquisite Narina Trogon. Its throaty call is easily mimicked, and an accurate echo of the male's hooting may coax it out of its hiding place in a brilliant burst of green, scarlet and white.

The challenge, then, is to actually see what is so often heard. But it is a pursuit where success is rare – and all the more rewarding for that rarity.

The cautious, but very vocal, Southern Boubou seldom ventures out from the tangled undergrowth it prefers. It skulks close to the ground in dense thickets, riverine bush and forest edges, foraging for insects, birds' eggs and fledglings.

A male Thickbilled Weaver binds 3 reed stems together with shredded bulrush leaves as the foundation for its nest. During the breeding season it commutes from reed bed to forest.

The Redfronted Tinker Barbet is so called for the scarlet blaze on its face that marks its maturity, and its clinking call, like a tiny hammer hitting an anvil. The little 'pot mender' feeds on fruit and on insects that it prises out from under loose bark.

A Little Sparrowhawk bathes in a pool. Easily overlooked, the small hawk is no bigger than a dove and frequents areas where the trees are tall and well canopied. It is remarkably adept at ambushing birds such as warblers, weavers and sunbirds.

The fruit-eating African Green Pigeon is almost parrot-like as it manoeuvres itself in trees, sometimes hanging upside down in its keen attempt to reach fruit. Although a wild fig is a particular delight, this bird relishes any fruit, wild or cultivated.

SERENADES IN THE WOODED KINGDOM

The Olive Thrush may not be a particularly striking forest bird as its plumage is fairly plain and unremarkable, but it boasts a fine singing voice which can be enjoyed in well-treed gardens and parks, where it is a common inhabitant. Prettier and less familiar, the Redthroated Twinspot communicates with an almost cricket-like rasp or a soft tinkling sound.

The thrush family are among the best songsters of the woods, having wonderfully eloquent and distinct voices. Birds that would otherwise go undetected in the brambled confusion of indigenous undergrowth, they announce their presence with high fluting trills, hooting and whistles – an exuberant and harmonious chorus.

Whether melodious or strident, there is an undefinable sweetness in the serenade of a bird you can't see.

The Redthroated Twinspot is wonderfully coloured, its black flanks decorated in an ordered profusion of white dots that look as though they have been freshly applied with a paintbrush. This quiet seed eater inhabits riverine forests in the far northeastern regions of southern Africa.

The widely distributed Olive Thrush, banqueting on a branch, is a common sight in gardens where it also pecks at the ground or among fallen leaves for insects, spiders and small lizards.

Coyly disguised by its plumage, the Knysna Lourie is well hidden in a tree, where it clambers about in a squirrel-like way. It may venture into well-wooded gardens and become quite tame. In flight, its crimson, black-tipped wing feathers contrast sharply with its viridian body.

The green of the Knysna Lourie's plumage comes from a unique pigment called turacoverdin, made in its own body. The red hue is derived from minute traces of copper in its diet. The presence of pigments produces another unusual feature in this bird – bright vermilion egg yolks!

The Purplecrested Lourie, like other louries, is a nimble and and noisy forest bird. It leaps and bounds in small active groups from branch to branch through leafy, fruited trees with great agility. It feeds mostly on fruit and buds from the higher branches.

BRIGHTLY PLUMED BIRDS THAT PLAY AMONG TREES

For birds of such vivid colour, it is surprising that Purple-crested Louries are not more conspicuous against the dense greenery of their habitat, especially as they dash and bound through trees in small hectic groups.

With frenetic shouting, high-pitched gobbling and even growling sounds, they crash through the upper canopy, running along boughs in an aerial game of tag. Their strong feet are equipped with a reversible outer toe that grips firmly onto branches, increasing their agility.

A fig tree attracts an intense buzz of activity among these birds, whose flashes of metallic purple and crimson show through the lacy network of the tree's foliage as they pick busily at this luscious fruit, a favourite among many fruit-eating birds.

Louries don't feed from the forest without playing some role in the continuing cycle of forest growth. When large-seeded fruit are swallowed, the seeds are regurgitated and dropped onto the ground to germinate and grow to feed another generation of the leaping and dancing birds.

It has been said that rain washes out a little of the red pigment that tinges the feathers of both the Knysna and Purplecrested Louries.
This does not, however, appear to be true. This Purplecrested Lourie lays its glossy white eggs on a flimsy platform of twigs built in a tree.

The crown that gives the Crowned Eagle its name is usually visible only when disturbed by wind or when the bird is excited. Although its dappled plumage makes it difficult to spot in the forest, its highly vocal flight displays above the canopy make it conspicuous in the air.

ROYAL HUNTER OF THE MIGHTY FOREST

The Crowned Eagle is an extremely daring and noble hunter, able to move with deadly stealth. Its feet, armed with formidable talons, are regarded by some as the most powerful of any bird of prey in Africa.

As still as stone the eagle scans the ground from a lofty perch, its mottled underparts merging into the woody background. A timid forest antelope moves beneath the watching eagle and instantly the raptor is upon it, enormous talons ripping into the startled creature's back.

The quarry is virtually squeezed to death in the vice-like grip of the shadowy hunter. The hind nail penetrates the body and the inside toe holds the prey while the bird rips off chunks of fur and flesh. So vital are the talons as killing tools that an eagle could starve to death if a leg were injured.

A Crowned Eagle pins the torn remains of its victim against a twisted bough and devours its prey, its crop noticeably distended. This powerful raptor is able to subdue an animal several times its own weight. Large kills may be dismembered and cached in trees.

A male African Paradise Flycatcher, his elegant tail feathers trailing, brings building material to his mate. The nest is a neat bowl of grass and roots delicately bound with spiders' webs and often built in a shady place over water. The eggs are creamy with a rusty rash at one end.

The eye ring and bill of the male African Paradise Flycatcher is a brighter blue than that of the female's. As its name implies, it feeds solely on insects, hawking at them in short flights from a perch, the long tail trailing behind it like an orange ribbon.

Ghostly and absolutely silent, a Wood Owl sets off into the night, the movement of its wings inaudible in the darkness. These monogamous night birds usually nest in a natural hole in a tree or in a partly hidden hollow on the ground.

If a Wood Owl dares to emerge from its rest before night falls, it risks being mobbed by angry smaller birds. A gentle and serene bird, it isn't easily panicked and will remain on its nest even when closely approached.

The Crested Guineafowl feeds on insects, arthropods, fruit and seeds, sometimes following a troop of monkeys for the fruit that they discard. Because of its rarity, this bird has not been considered a game bird and, unlike the Helmeted Guineafowl, has been protected from hunters.

CURLY-HEADED GUINEAFOWL ALL IN A ROW

There is an almost endearing quality about the Crested Guineafowl, the curly black topknot adorning its head being its most distinguishing feature. Boasting button-bright red eyes and impeccably patterned plumage, the Crested Guineafowl is more rare and secretive than the popular and well-known Helmeted Guineafowl.

It skulks about nervously in dense thickets and on the edge of evergreen forests in the far northeastern parts of the country, but may venture into the open in a straggling row of neatly dotted birds.

With its heavy body and proportionately small head, it does not seem to be ideally designed for flight, but it flies up to high branches if disturbed, and to reach limbs on which it roosts communally. It prefers, however, to stay close to the ground, scratching in the earth and among leaves for food.

The nest of the impeccably spotted Crested Guineafowl is a simple scrape on the ground, thinly layered with plant material and positioned in thick undergrowth or next to an exposed clump of tree roots. The fledgling uses its bill to climb and manoeuvre itself before it can fly.

The African Goshawk hunts from a concealed position but is a conservative hunter and carefully judges the size of its quarry before trying to overpower it. The female is far larger and heavier than the male but depends on him to feed her and the chicks when she is nesting.

The Forest Buzzard is often confused with the more widely spread and commonly seen Steppe Buzzard. This bird of prey is mostly confined to the indigenous forests along the southeastern coastal plain. Although it has adapted to exotic forests, this may be a species under threat.

WILD DANCES OF FREEDOM

The raptors that inhabit the forests must rely on strong wings and great agility to manoeuvre through trees and foliage as they hunt. But it is not a habitat that allows extravagant and lengthy flights, so these creatures of the air often escape their leafy confines to soar in spectacular, undulating displays of aerial showmanship. The courtship flights of some species are especially dramatic.

The African Goshawk, for example, flies high above its forest habitat, performing its aerial display and making a sharp call that can be heard over a considerable distance.

The relay race to quell insatiable appetites

When birds have young in the nest, their lives become more stressful than usual. Not only do they have to feed themselves, they also have to provide food for their growing offspring. Constant feeding is crucial in the first few days of a nestling's life – in that short time it will either grow enough to set it on the path to adulthood, or it will die.

But despite the parents' marathon efforts, nature will ensure that only the fittest survive. The smaller nestlings in a brood often perish, particularly when food is scarce. In some species, however, smaller birds are threatened even when food is plentiful. The first-hatched of some birds, such as egrets and large eagles, for example, will fight any smaller sibling and kill it – a harsh solution that will nevertheless ensure the survival of at least one nestling.

Some nestlings, like those of egrets, stay in the nest until they are able to fly, whereas those of many ground nesters, such as francolins and waders, leave the nest soon after hatching to fend for themselves.

Pearlbreasted Swallow nestlings gape as one of their parents soars up to the nest. The gape is a begging action which the adult bird cannot ignore, and nestlings must use it to be fed.

Even a whole frog will not satisfy a Cattle Egret chick for long; it will soon be calling desperately for more food. The colour of the parent's beak is important to chicks: the bill of the Great White Egret, for example, changes from yellow to black at the onset of the breeding season.

AN EXPLOSION OF ACTIVITY

As though a switch has been flicked, a clutch of nestlings suddenly rears their bald heads held unsteadily on scrawny necks. Each chick stretches as high as possible, chirps frantically, opens its beak as wide as it can and flaps its stubby wings madly to attract attention.

The activity has been triggered by the vibration created by one of their parents alighting on the edge of the nest, and it will end only when the last of the young is replete. When

A cuckoo nestling as large as its foster parent amply fills the Cape Batis' nest in which it hatched. The huge gape of the young bird ensures that it gets the food it requires. A gape of such a size is a supernormal stimulus, often to the detriment of the young in nearby nests.

food is plentiful, the parents feed the gaping mouths random-
ly but when it is scarce, the stronger nestlings get preference.

Some species have found a way of cheating on the high
energy needs of rearing a brood. These birds, called brood
parasites, lay their eggs in the nests of birds of a different
species, relying on the host parents to feed and raise the
parasitic youngsters.

Cuckoos are well-studied brood parasites. Soon after
hatching, cuckoo chicks push all the other eggs out of the
nest, ensuring they get their foster parents' sole attention.

*The number of adults engaged in feeding the young varies greatly. For instance, only the parents will feed these Bokmakierie nestlings,
whereas the nestlings of the gregarious Chestnutfronted Shrike, which lives in groups of up to 10 when breeding, are fed by all the adults.*

DEADLY SIBLINGS AND THEIR FIGHT TO SURVIVE

The young of raptors usually hatch with a full covering of down and with their eyes open. The first-hatched Verreaux's Eagle chick, older than its sibling by only three or four days, invariably kills its younger and smaller sibling by pecking repeatedly at its head, or starving it to death by monopolizing the food brought to the nest – a phenomenon known as Cainism.

Even though a single nestling now occupies the nest, its appetite remains voracious and keeping it fed is a full-time job. In areas where the staple prey of Verreaux's Eagles is dassies, the parents, hunting for themselves and for their nestling, will kill an average of one dassie a day, which they tear apart to feed to the nestling; smaller prey is consumed whole. Other prey includes hares, monkeys and smaller birds such as doves.

The number of trips the parents make is set by the size of the prey: the larger it is, the fewer the number of trips the parents need to make.

Innocently white and fluffy, a Verreaux's Eagle nestling will have killed its younger sibling to ensure its parents' undivided attention.

Standing out from the gloom in which their nests are built – under culverts, eaves and overhanging rock formations – the light-coloured rims and glistening pink of the mouths of Pearlbreasted Swallows await their meal of insects, like a row of carnivorous flowers.

Bank Cormorants regurgitate food when the nestling plunges its head into its parent's beak. Adult cormorants may be kept busy feeding chicks all year when food supplies are abundant, since in these conditions breeding takes place throughout the year on the same nest.

The Barn Owl is a consummate hunter and the farmer's friend – a pair has been recorded catching at least 24 mice in just less than 18 minutes to feed 7 nestlings. When food is abundant the female lays as many as 12 eggs and, when it is scarce, as few as 3.

THE NEED FOR NEST HYGIENE

Nestlings produce large amounts of waste. In many species this is removed by the parents and dropped some distance away. This keeps the nest and surrounding areas clean and also prevents an accumulation of droppings or faecal sacs (young nestlings produce their waste in these gelatinous envelopes) that may reveal the nest's position to predators.

Other species such as the Bank Cormorant may use the same nest for a year or more and do not remove the nestlings' waste. Hence, the nest and surrounding area is soon liberally covered in guano.

But the most notorious species is the Hoopoe. It removes neither droppings nor old eggshells and its nest soon smells bad enough to deter all but the most resolute predator. The young reinforce the deterrent odour of the nest by spraying liquid excreta at predators and producing a vile-smelling secretion from the preen gland.

Providing a meal on the wing by feeding an insect larva to a nestling that sticks its neck out of the nest entrance may seem a clean and tidy way of eating, but Hoopoes' nests themselves are notoriously filthy and foul smelling.

Hunters and gatherers of the African highveld

The grassland of southern Africa, known to many as the 'highveld', is a vast expanse that centres on the high-lying plateau of the southeastern interior. Yet it is a habitat that varies greatly, from the stunted scrub of the flat plains to the scarred cliff faces and dramatic peaks of the high montane grassland in the misty belt of the Drakensberg escarpment. Where the wheaten-coloured fields extend up gentle slopes and drape the foothills of the Maluti Mountains, the uncluttered simplicity of the undulating horizon is breathtaking.

Of all the world's biomes, grassland is the most arable and, like the Argentinian pampas, American prairie and Eurasian steppe, many millions of hectares have succumbed to the insidious and relentless encroachment of humans. Where herds of black wildebeest once roamed, there is now a patchwork of cultivated lands and sprawling cities.

However, though the unstoppable advance of farmland and plantations has radically reduced the range of such ecologically sensitive bird species as the Wattled Crane – now on the endangered list – other species have coped well with the upheaval caused by agriculture in their natural habitats, and now create some havoc of their own. The monotonous stretches of mielie fields and other single-grain crops offer food in such easily accessible abundance, that they sometimes attract Red Queleas in huge numbers which blacken the sky like swarms of locusts.

This mostly treeless region is home to many elusive terrestrial birds. Inconspicuous in habit and hue, they gain some shelter from predators by their subdued colours as they search among grassy tufts for bulbs, ground fruit and snails. Francolins and quails are typical of these secretive ground feeders, skulking in growing crops, and loudly proclaiming their presence at dusk in vocalizations ranging from melodic song to grating discord. The African Quail seldom flies, nesting and feeding on the ground and frantically taking to the air only when it is very closely approached.

And then there are the smaller feathered veld dwellers that flit busily over long grasses. Hardly distinguishable from one another as they scuttle and dash among spiky tufts and termite mounds, these often dull-coloured, barely noticeable birds are characteristic of the grassland. They include pipits, larks and cisticolas.

The drab Orangethroated Longclaw does make one concession to style. While maintaining a subdued khaki shade on its upper parts to camouflage itself from aerial hunters, it flashes a tangerine belly in flight, enhancing the surprising display by fanning its white-tipped tail. Its alarm call is a piercing catlike mewing sound, usually given during its peculiar bouncing flight.

The Secretarybird, sometimes referred to as the Terrestrial Eagle for its remarkable hunting prowess, is one of the bolder

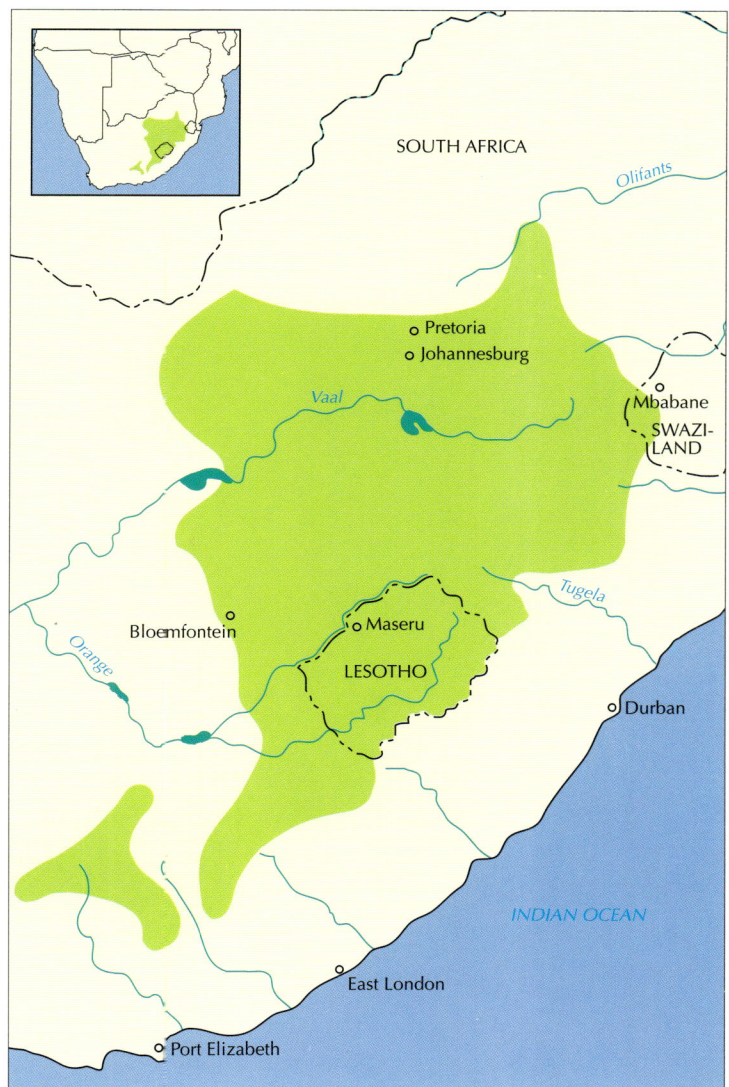

GRASSLANDS

The Wattled Plover is named for the yellow flaps, or wattles, on either side of its beak. They are used in the courtship ritual.

The Rufousnaped Lark often perches on vantage points such as fence posts, rocks or termite mounds when calling. It sometimes imitates other bird calls.

The Orangethroated Longclaw is a common sight in the grassland and is so named for the extremely long claw on the hind toe. The function of its awkward big feet is not clearly understood, but this little insect eater nevertheless manages to perch on the most slender of branches.

and more visually prominent residents of the grassland. It feeds on anything that it can overpower, including snakes, rodents and nestlings. The fairly tame Southern Crowned Crane breeds in marshland but enjoys feeding on fallen grain in freshly ploughed fields.

The grassland is also the range of many birds that actually live in the mountains, but descend onto this fertile land for food. The widely ranging Lanner Falcon, for example, sweeps in across the veld to prey on reptiles, small mammals, and even terrestrial birds. A bustling young francolin is easy prey to this soaring predator which dives from out of the sky to snatch it from the ground in a breathless second. Unlike these birds, the rare and endangered Bearded Vulture is restricted to the high cliffs of Lesotho and the Drakensberg.

iSakabuli, or the Longtailed Widow, is another true bird of the grassland. The black male of the species is instantly recognizable by the long floppy tail that hangs heavily behind it. The low choppy flight of this seed eater as it leaves its post on a farm fence is a familiar sight on a long stretch of road. After breeding, the male loses its distinctive tail and its sooty blackness and reverts to the brown shade of its mate.

The highveld's climate is marked by hot summers, when the heat is relieved only by dramatic and violent thunderstorms, and cold dry winters during which the parched vegetation is periodically ravaged by fires. A number of birds are attracted to these, being quite partial to feeding in the charred stubble. Included in their numbers are species such as the Wattled Plover and the White Stork. The Southern Bald Ibis, too, will leave its colony on a high mountainside to forage in the burnt winter grass. Conspicuous with its white face and red bill, it follows in the fire's wake, stepping across crackling black tufts and probing the warm, soft ground for food, turning over clods and dung for insects – dead or alive – and feeding on the carcasses of any rodents that have fallen victim to the flames.

A Bearded Vulture is said to have killed the Greek poet Aeschylus by dropping a tortoise onto his bald head circa 456 BC. The tale may be apocryphal, being fuelled by this magnificent raptor's unique habit of breaking the bones of prey by dropping them on flat rocks.

A VALUABLE FAMILY UNDER THREAT

Carrion eaters perform a vital role in the wild by consuming animal remains that might otherwise spread disease, but some of these birds are under threat and their numbers are declining, as are their ranges.

The Cape Vulture population, for instance, is being steadily reduced. Some of the main reasons include the use of pesticides in agriculture, reduced game populations and the bird's slow breeding rate, combined with deaths through electrocution (these birds often use electricity pylons as nesting sites). The Cape Vulture is an efficient feeder when it is at a carcass: its grooved tongue that is serrated along the edge enables the bird to feed very quickly, removing and swallowing as much as a kilogram of flesh in a few minutes.

The Egyptian Vulture (which throws rocks at Ostrich eggs to break them so that it can reach the contents) is a good example of a species that has declined. Once seen over much of southern Africa this bird is now very rare and it is believed that only one or two breeding pairs survive in remote parts of Namibia.

The red-brown colour of this Bearded Vulture's breast plumage comes from dust-bathing in soils rich in iron oxide. This individual is perched on an ossuary – a flat rock on which the bird drops bones too large to swallow so that they shatter into smaller, more manageable pieces.

People often associate the Secretarybird with snakes, marvelling at this bird's ability to attack the lethal reptiles. In fact, they make up only a tiny proportion of its diet. Grasshoppers and other insects are by far the largest source of nutrition for these birds.

The Secretarybird's name is derived from the Arabic word saqr-et-tair, meaning 'hunter-bird'. It differs from other raptors in hunting only on the ground, stamping on rodents, lizards and snakes to kill them. It swallows snakes whole.

Abdim's Stork is an intra-African migrant – it is the only stork in southern Africa that does not breed here. These highly gregarious birds roost in huge numbers and form large flocks when they migrate. They breed in sub-Saharan Africa north of the Equator.

The White Stork breeds in a limited area near Bredasdorp in South Africa, in North Africa and in Europe, its main breeding region. There, however, it has lost much of its range through human encroachment, and the effects of chemicals and pollution.

Its Afrikaans name, Langstertflap, describes the Longtailed Widow's flight most aptly – laboured flapping of broad wings, long tail dangling to entice a mate. Experiments in Kenya showed that artificially lengthening the male's tail increased its attractiveness to females.

FLAMBOYANT POLYGAMISTS

The Longtailed Widow and Cape Weaver are both members
of the family that includes sparrows, bishops, queleas and
the Cuckoo Finch – all granivorous, in that they are grain and
seed eaters, and typical of grassland.

Except for the sparrows, the males in these species don
bright or distinctive plumage during the breeding season to
attract the females. The Cape Weaver loses his winter drab-
ness and becomes bright yellow, while the Longtailed Widow
gains tail feathers of extravagant length.

Both have a flamboyant display flight, the Widow's
being so conspicuous that it can be seen from a kilometre
away, while the Weaver performs an aerial dance close to
the nest that it is advertising.

Both birds are polygynous, moving from one female
to the next, once each one has been successfully courted –
the Longtailed Widow may have up to 6 females in a season.

Where you find water in grassland, you will almost certainly find the Cape Weaver. This is a breeding male, as evidenced by its brownish-orange face and black bill. When not breeding, the bill becomes brown and the brownish-orange hue becomes a greyish-olive colour.

Lanner Falcons are more adaptable when it comes to nesting sites than, say, Peregrine Falcons. In addition to cliffs, they also nest on power-line pylons. One pair nested in an 8th-floor windowbox in Harare, Zimbabwe, where they preyed on the city's pigeon population.

ADAPT AND PROSPER

As has been shown time and again, those animals that can adapt are the ones that prosper. Many birds are facing increasing encroachment from agriculture and expanding cities, and their breeding and feeding ranges are steadily getting smaller.

Lanner Falcons, however, have learned to live near humans and in doing so, now help to contain the pigeon and rodent populations in built-up areas.

Lanner Falcons sometimes hunt in teams of 2 or more individuals, one bird flushing out other, smaller birds as prey so that the rest of the team can take them on the wing. In hunting co-operatively like this, these birds emulate some pack hunters in the wild.

The Southern Crowned Crane found locally is one of the most striking of the crane family, which is found worldwide and is highly regarded by many peoples. In the Far East, Redcrowned Cranes are symbols of longevity and good luck, and are often depicted in Japanese art.

Apart from its distinctive straw-coloured crest, the Southern Crowned Crane differs from other members of the crane family in its habit of roosting in trees and sometimes even on electricity pylons. These birds tend to breed in wetlands, but feed in grassland and cultivated fields.

SUCCESSFUL, BUT NOT COMPLETELY SAFE

Ibises as a group are successful birds around the globe, and four species thrive in southern Africa – the Sacred Ibis, the Glossy Ibis, the Hadeda and the Southern Bald Ibis. The last was once more widespread in southern Africa, but the influence of agriculture and natural factors led to a decline in the species' numbers. It is now relatively rare in the region, with a population of only 5 000 or so.

The damage caused by human beings is probably the main reason for the decline in the numbers of some bird species. Birds often manage to survive even the most severe natural disasters, which, as they are often of relatively short duration, allow the species to recover. But human influences are usually permanent. The Southern Bald Ibis, for example, is losing its feeding areas to agriculture and unless it can adapt, or encroachment is curtailed, the species might again go into a decline – this time never to recover.

It is significant that its young eat large numbers of maize stalk borers – a major pest that costs farmers a great deal to combat. Southern Bald Ibises do the job for free.

The Southern Bald Ibis is a communal cliff rooster, though it also roosts in trees. Each nest, a simple platform of sticks on a ledge under a protective overhang, may be very close to its neighbours – unlike some species which have to space their nests according to pecking range.

The Southern Bald Ibis sometimes forages for scorched insects after a veld fire, but its usual diet comprises snails, small mammals, birds and frogs. It searches for the roasted morsels by turning over leaves and cow pats, using its long beak with quick, decisive movements.

The Rock Kestrel, like the Lanner Falcon, is adaptable and can be found in grassland, arid savannah, deserts – and towns. They are solitary birds which tend to prey on small rodents, reptiles and insects.

A Rock Kestrel hangs motionless in the air, often hovering until it spots its prey. It then descends in a series of parachuting swoops until contact is made. Ground prey is preferred but it can also take birds in flight.

The Cattle Egret is a highly successful wanderer. In 1937 it spread from Africa to South America, subsequently moving into the southern part of North America, and by 1948 it had reached northern Australia. By 1963 it had made sporadic appearances in New Zealand.

Cattle Egrets are highly gregarious birds and congregate in large flocks near their nesting and breeding sites. They nest in mixed colonies in reed beds, often with cormorants, ibises and other herons. Besides foraging for insects, tney also fish in shallow water.

HOME ON THE RANGE

The Cattle Egret is also known as the Tick Bird, perhaps because it is so often seen perched on the backs of grazing animals and in the vicinity of game. Only a very small portion of its diet, however, is made up of ticks. Indeed, the reason for associating so closely with cattle, as its name implies, is that the slow grazing of these domestic animals flushes insects out so effectively that foraging independently would hardly be worth the bird's while.

Small groups of Cattle Egrets are a common sight on recently ploughed land, where they feed on soil creatures such as grasshoppers, beetles and caterpillars. Occasionally they will eat small reptiles and mammals as well.

The Cattle Egret has adapted so well to cultivated lands and farms where herds of cattle roam that its range has expanded throughout the warmer parts of the world.

The Jackal Buzzard's very broad wings meet the tail when fully spread and present an ideal surface that allows this species to ride rising air currents over hills and cliffs, watching for prey. It feeds on birds, rats, carrion, road kills and reptiles – even snakes such as puff adders.

Birds are the favourite prey of the Peregrine Falcon, which pursues them with astounding speed and catches them in flight with its hind claws. This is an elusive bird which perches for long periods on cliff ledges before swooping across grassland and wooded areas to hunt.

Ingenious architects and house-proud home builders

One bird glues its nest and its eggs to a palm frond. Another creates a tiny cuplike masterpiece of grass, spiders' webs and lichen. For some birds, a shallow depression simply scraped out of the ground is sufficient. Others build huge communal nests as big as haystacks.

When is a nest a nest? The simple answer is, when the bird thinks it is – whether it is a floating pile of sticks or an elaborate honeycomb construction that took weeks to build.

Foiling predators is often a prime objective in the way nests are constructed. Sociable Weavers create a wall of spikes in the tunnel entrance of each nest in their huge communal nests. This deters almost every predator, except for cobras and boomslangs, which remain an ever-present threat.

Cape Penduline Tits build their baglike nests on the extreme ends of the thinnest twigs. The safety of their young is ensured by a special feature – a false entrance that leads to a cul-de-sac, fooling predators into thinking the nest is empty. Below it, however, is the real entrance – an invisible, cleverly constructed slit that has to be forced open and then springs shut behind the bird.

South African Cliff Swallows use small pellets of mud, stuck together like bricks, to create a nest rather like a jar. Over time hundreds of these nests may be built, creating a colony, often under a bridge or culvert.

Serried ranks of South African Cliff Swallows' nests are spaced with perfect regularity according to the birds' pecking range.

A South African Cliff Swallow hangs upside down and vibrates his wings to attract a mate. When he finally does find a partner, he and the female will recognise each other by their voices – an incredible feat in a colony that could be home to as many as 900 birds.

The underside of a Sociable Weaver nest is a maze of entrances protected by nipped-off straw, angled inwards to deter predators. Some of these communal nests may be as much as 7 m across, remarkable for a bird that weighs about 27 g, and have been in use for over 100 years.

Unlike those of other weavers, a Redheaded Weaver's nest is untidy – as is already evident in this one still under construction. These birds build their nests in inaccessible places, on telephone wires for example, where they are much safer from attack by predators such as snakes.

A Thickbilled Weaver's nest is revealed to potential mates when the male, the architect of the nest, strips foliage off surrounding reeds.

THE SKILL OF THE MASTER BUILDERS

There is a wide range of beautifully crafted nests in the avian world, some of the most impressive being those constructed by many of the weaver species.

First the male weaver constructs a ring of grass and palm fronds, using his beak and feet to weave lengths of the material together. This ring is the foundation for a nest with which he hopes to attract a mate. If she rejects the nest, he tears it apart and starts all over again. In a study of one Masked Weaver, it built 204 nests over a period of 8 years. Of these, 24 were acceptable and used for breeding, but in only 17 were young raised successfully.

Flycatchers and batises build some of the most exquisite nests in the avian kingdom. Their tiny cup-shaped creations are bound with cobwebs and covered in lichen or bark to camouflage them. The Whitetailed Flycatcher uses moss in its nest and binds extra material into a Y-shaped stalk which makes the finished nest resemble a green wine glass.

Some nests don't even resemble nests at all. The Palm Swift, for example, uses saliva to glue a vertical pad of feathers to a palm frond and then glues its eggs to the pad. Such a construction may even hang vertically so that when the chicks hatch they have to use their well-developed claws to hold on to it until they are able to fly.

Having finished its nest, a male Yellow Weaver sets out to entice a female to set up home with him.

During the incubation period, a female Chinspot Batis seldom leaves her nest and has to rely on her mate to provide her with food. Spiders' webs are used to bind the nest together.

Filthy but functional, a Whitebreasted Cormorant's nest is a crude platform of sticks constructed on the ground, a cliff, a rocky island or in a tree. The nest is often re-used year after year, becoming thickly encrusted with guano. This acts like a cement and strengthens the nest.

A well-camouflaged nest provides relative security for this trio of ravenous African Paradise Flycatcher chicks while their parents are away gathering food. The lichen used in the construction of this nest helps it merge with the branches on which it has been built.

Winged creatures of the woodland wilderness

A thin swathe of green wilderness begins in a remote desert grove of maroelas, makalani and wild fig trees around Etosha Pan and stretches eastwards to the tall and lush miombo woodlands that flourish on the Zimbabwean plateau.

Skirting the parched Kalahari heartland, dense thickets of thorn trees and mopanes grow in the Limpopo valley, and extend in patches of untamed *bundu* along the eastern edge of the country. This beloved African bushveld, shrill with the sound of cicadas, weaves around true forest and grassland until it finally surrenders to the Karoo plains in the south.

Characterized by deciduous trees that grow in varying degrees of denseness and scrubby patches of tangled bushes, with the ground beneath the leafy canopy usually being well grassed, the woodlands of southern Africa form an extravagantly varied mosaic of rich and diverse habitats.

This wild country offers shade from the African sun, ample food, water and shelter, and supports game as well as a great variety of bird life.

Mixed flocks of rollers, shrikes and starlings feed together on the generous supply of insects that inhabit the dense vegetation.

The birds foraging on the ground cause insects to burst out of their grassy cover only to be caught by the birds in the trees. Feeding in large numbers like this may offer some protection from predators who are less likely to surprise an active flock than one distracted bird.

While the abundance of fruit and flowers in some areas attracts sunbirds and louries, the opportunistic Yellowbilled Oxpecker is drawn by large animals like the buffalo and giraffe. The bird props itself up on its stiff tail to pull blood-engorged ticks from an animal's hide, placidly tolerated by the grazing beast. The use of dips and slow decline of game have drastically reduced the range of the oxpecker and it is mostly confined to game parks.

The solitary Bateleur, a hunter and scavenger, also finds safe harbour in bushveld reserves. Its population has been much reduced in many areas where carcasses are deliberately poisoned by farmers in an attempt to control jackals and other small carnivores.

Most of the woodland birds are tree dwellers, building nests that range from the finely moulded cups of the Chinspot Batis to the unwieldy bowl of sticks of the Marabou Stork. There are nests that hang from leafy branches and those that are simply wedged into the fork of a tree. Some are open, others are almost entirely sealed.

Dead trees provide good nesting opportunities for those arboreal birds that are equipped to 'drill' or peck holes into wood to create a space to nest in. The Crested Barbet, a

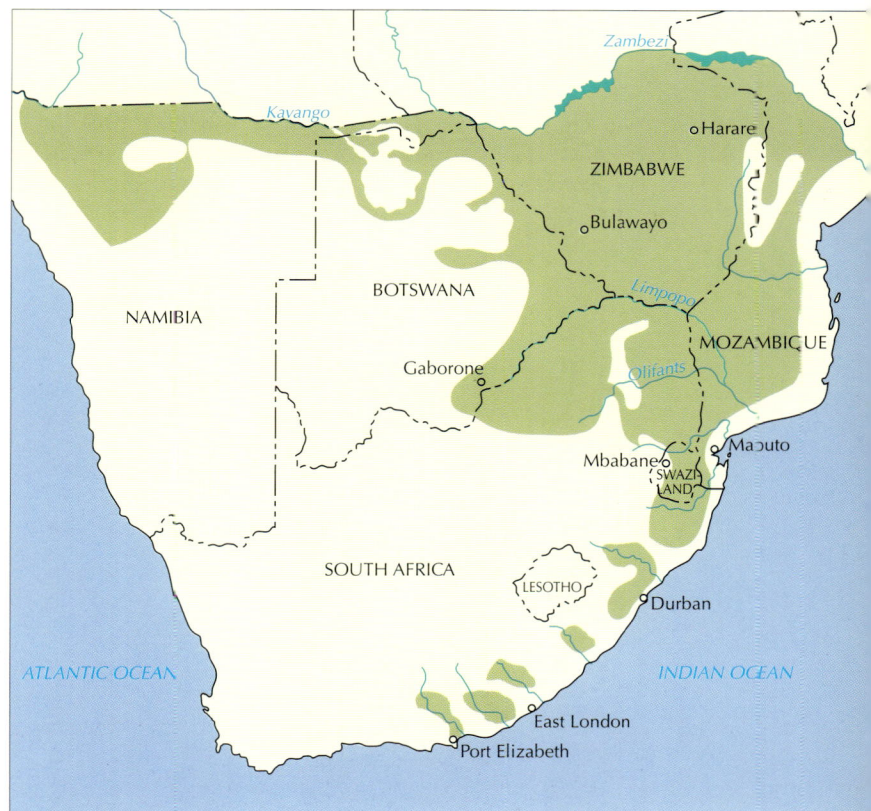

The huge bill of the Southern Yellowbilled Hornbill is supported by fused neck vertebrae as well as strong neck muscles.

EASTERN WOODLANDS

The Yellowbilled Oxpecker's most important hosts are the Cape buffalo and the giraffe, but this bird is declining throughout southern Africa because lower game populations and dipping of domestic cattle to combat ticks are reducing its preferred food – ticks and other parasites.

common garden visitor, excavates a hole into the brittle wood of a well-rotted tree at the start of its breeding season. Although it is enormously curious about its neighbours and peers inquisitively into every nest or hole it chances on, this bird brooks no intrusion into its own territory. It defends its nest fiercely, scolding trespassers furiously with a sustained trill that has been compared to a ringing alarm clock without the bell cover.

Like cuckoos, honeyguides are brood parasites, often stealing into other birds' nests to surreptitiously add their eggs to the clutch, and the Lesser Honeyguide is particularly partial to the nest of the Blackcollared Barbet. It constantly harangues and harasses the bird and, at the first opportunity, lays its eggs in the distracted barbet's nest. It then abandons them there, relinquishing any further parental responsibilities.

The Southern Yellowbilled Hornbill, widely distributed in bushveld and arid thornveld – particularly where acacia trees grow – is also a hole nester. It selects crevices in trees or rocks, often taking over a previously used nest site. All hornbills, apart from the Southern Ground Hornbill, have the peculiar distinction of being the only birds whose incubating female seals herself into the nest. The breeding season of these omnivorous birds coincides with the onset of summer rains when there is plenty of mud available. The female incarcerates herself in the nest, carefully plastering and sealing off the entrance with a mixture of mud, droppings and wood bark brought to her by the male. She pats and smooths the material in place with her large bill, leaving a small, barely perceptible slit through which the male will feed her throughout her incubation. Thus concealed and safe from predation, she lays her eggs and begins the next stage of her breeding cycle. She undergoes a complete moult and will break out of the hole only once she has regained her feathers and the nestlings are half grown.

Like many birds of the woodlands, the Southern Yellowbilled Hornbill is sociable and quite vocal, the clucking call of one bird setting off a whole group.

The Southern Ground Hornbill gives a low-pitched, booming call that sounds more like a lion in the distance than a bird, a disconcerting sound in the bushveld dawn.

The raucous call of the Hadeda Ibis as it flaps overhead in large flocks is a familiar sound in many parts of southern Africa. Besides the bushveld and woodlands, its range includes most of the country except for the dry regions of the interior and the west. According to the early inhabitants of KwaZulu-Natal, the flight cry of the ibis, or *iNkankane*, is 'ngahamba, ngahamba' (I travel, I travel).

The parts of the African bushveld that are still untamed and unspoilt offer sanctuary to bird and beast, they deserve to be honoured and conserved with impeccable care before there is nowhere left to remind us of what that wild freedom was all about.

The territorial Crested Barbet is often associated with dead trees in mopane woodlands and is a notoriously compulsive wood 'borer'.

A Grey Lourie raises its crest in alarm. Though these birds eat flowers, buds, leaves, seeds, insects and even other nesting birds, this species is primarily a fruit eater. They are very vocal and their distinctive call 'go-'way' has led to them being called the Goaway Bird.

The Speckled Mousebird gets its name from the rodent-like way it clambers about bushes and trees looking for fruit, seeds, palatable leaves, nectar – and the occasional insect. Its fast flight often ends in a clumsy and inelegant landing as it crashes into a bush or a tree.

THE WOODWORKERS

The woodpecker is the avian world's specialist woodworker and is well equipped to make short work of just about any kind of wood.

Its chisel-tipped bill is mounted on a strong bony skull that is cushioned by muscles so that it can take the shock of the pecking action. Clawed toes give a good grip on tree bark, and a stiffened tail, pressed firmly against the tree, enables the bird to use maximum force against the wood.

The holes these birds excavate are often used by other species which are unable to make their own – such as hornbills. However, worldwide deforestation is reducing the number of suitable trees and, consequently, some woodpecker species face extinction. As a result, other birds, such as hornbills and toucans, that often depend on woodpeckers to excavate nesting holes, are also threatened.

The bill of the Bennett's Woodpecker is not as robust as that of some other woodpecker species and it therefore prefers to nest in existing holes in tree trunks, though it will enlarge or excavate a hole if necessary. The eggs are laid on a bed of wood chips.

Redbilled Hornbills lay a clutch of 4 or 5 eggs, which are incubated only by the female, which seals herself in the nest until about 20 days after the first egg has hatched. At that time, she breaks the seal and leaves the nest, which the nestlings then reseal.

The female Laughing Dove builds a flimsy nest from material brought by the male and usually lays 2 eggs. After the young have hatched, the remains of the shells are taken by the adults and dropped some distance away, presumably to avoid drawing attention to the nest.

THE MILK-PRODUCING BIRDS

Pigeons and doves, of which there are 304 species, belong to the same family. The term 'pigeon' is generally used for the larger species and 'dove' for the smaller ones.

As a family of birds they are not perhaps as spectacular as some, especially those that include the sunbirds or the large raptors, but they are most interesting in that they produce crop milk – a cheesy, protein-rich substance which is also referred to as 'pigeon's milk'.

When the birds are breeding, special glands in the crops of both the males and the females enlarge and secrete this thick, milky substance, which is then fed to the young.

Like many birds, Laughing Doves sunbathe and seem to enjoy the sensation. Sunbathing probably has several functions, one of which might be that the heat of the sun's rays causes parasites to move about, so making them easier for the preening bird to remove.

The prominent wattles, large helmet and extensive amount of bare skin on the head of the Helmeted Guineafowl are believed to help the bird regulate the temperature of its brain in different weather conditions. The helmet is also known as a 'casque'.

The Helmeted Guineafowl is widely distributed over southern Africa, particularly favouring areas where water is available. Farmers welcome this species on their lands as it feeds on insects that are regarded as pests.

MAKING THE MOST OF MAN-MADE STRUCTURES

The use of electricity pylons as nesting platforms has helped increase the range of some eagle species, particularly where a lack of suitable nesting sites in trees has inhibited nest building. There has even been a case of a pair of Martial Eagles leaving a tree site for a newly erected pylon nearby. Tawny Eagles, however, seldom use pylons as nesting sites.

Its head feathers wet with rain, a Tawny Eagle displays its dangerously hooked beak. It is a pirate and an opportunistic carrion feeder, but it is also very partial to termites, gathering with other birds to consume large numbers of them as they mill about on the ground after rain.

If food remains plentiful, Tawny Eagles will occupy the same territory and nest in the same area for many years. They usually build their nest at the top of a thorn tree, but on rare occasions they will use an electricity pylon as a nesting site.

It may be dubbed by some as the 'world's ugliest bird', but the Marabou Stork's white undertail coverts are so beautiful that they were once used by milliners to adorn hats. These feathers are known as 'marabou down'.

THE MARVELLOUS MARABOU

Marabou Storks are among the most unprepossessing of any bird species. They are also among the most opportunistic and versatile birds when it comes to feeding.

Their varied diet allows them to make use of a wide range of situations. For instance, even though this large bird eats carrion and refuse, it also preys on insects, rodents, birds (even adult flamingos) and a wide range of aquatic creatures such as fish, frogs – and young crocodiles.

Favourite feeding opportunities are shrinking pools heavily stocked with fish.

Marabou Storks urinate on their legs to cool them. When the urine dries, it leaves a layer of white uric acid crystals which give the legs their customary white colour – even though they are naturally black.

Lilacbreasted Rollers provide a startling splash of colour as they perch on the tops of trees, bushes or on telephone wires, from which they can view their surroundings. They are attracted to veld fires where they wait on the edges to catch insects fleeing the flames.

Little Bee-eaters nest in burrows about 500 mm long with a nesting chamber at the end. A small lip at the opening prevents any eggs from rolling out and being lost. The burrows are often made in the wall or roof of an aardvark's hole.

THE CALL OF THE WILD

Some birds modify their alarm calls so as to make the caller difficult to locate. For example, the '*seet*' call of a European Chaffinch (of which there is a small population in the Cape) warns its fellows of a hawk overhead. However, it is not a constant note and waxes and wanes – making it difficult to pinpoint the position of the calling bird. In contrast, the '*chink*' call, used to warn of a ground predator such as a cat, can be located, and gives other birds the prowler's position.

The noisy Hadeda Ibis is often found in gardens, using its long beak to probe the soil for earthworms and crickets and to forage over the surface for insects. If disturbed it takes off with a series of loud 'haaas' and sometimes lands next door to continue feeding.

The Lappetfaced Vulture, also called the King Vulture, dominates any gathering at a carcass and easily repels other raptors. Its bill is the most formidable of any raptor and enables it to open even the toughest hide. This bird occasionally calls in a shrill whistle.

The Brownhooded Kingfisher does fish, albeit inexpertly and not very often. Usually it feeds on insects, small birds and reptiles.

A solitary Greyhooded Kingfisher would rather sit on its branch, waiting for a small lizard or insect such as a grasshopper or beetle to make an appearance on the ground below, than fish in river waters. Many of the kingfisher family hunt this way.

The brightly coloured Pygmy Kingfisher migrates to southern Africa from tropical Africa, arriving in October and leaving in April. During its migrations, it flies at night – which sometimes results in it flying into buildings and being stunned or even killed.

The Barn Owl's flight is almost silent because its feathers are covered with a velvet-like pile that dampens sound. Although it preys mainly on rodents, this widely distributed owl will also hunt for birds, deliberately disturbing roosting birds by beating bushes.

The Wood Owl's eyesight, about 35 times more acute than ours, matches that of the Barn Owl. It hunts nocturnally and can spot its prey from a great distance on even the darkest night. This mouse probably did not even see or hear the bird before being caught.

The Southern Ground Hornbill with its red wattles and bare face is also called the Turkey Buzzard, although it is related to neither. Females have bluish wattles. This bird has a peculiar way of walking on its toes as it stalks over the veld. Its booming call is mostly heard at dawn.

DUAL-PURPOSE WATTLES

The prominent wattles of many species of birds are often their most striking feature, in that they may change colour during courtship or when the bird is under threat.

They are also believed to serve another purpose, however – as temperature regulators. Being bare of plumage and well supplied with blood, they act like radiators and lose heat quickly to the atmosphere. This helps the bird to keep comfortably cool in hot weather.

When roosting at night, the sleeping bird tucks its head under a wing where the wattles will be insulated and heat loss will be minimized.

Even from the rear, large red wattles are clearly visible on this Southern Ground Hornbill. It is a carnivore and forages on the ground for frogs, snails, insects, mammals and reptiles – including tortoises. It also takes snakes, usually with the help of other members of the group.

ROLLERS – AERIAL ACROBATS

The name of this family is derived from the males' very distinctive and vigorous display flights. These comprise a complex series of somersaults, rolls, tumbles and loops and are complemented by the species' loud and raucous calls, which are repeated again and again. These actions, combined with the birds' bright colours, make them most conspicuous.

They defend their territories aggressively. Broadbilled Rollers drive away other members of the same species and even harass raptors that get too close.

The small hook on the end of the upper beak enables these birds to catch a wide variety of woodland creatures, from insects, their main prey, to the larger inhabitants such as rodents, young birds, scorpions and reptiles.

The bright yellow of its beak sets the Broadbilled Roller apart from other southern African rollers. It is more commonly found in denser bushveld and tall woodlands, where it prefers to feed at dusk, hunting from a high perch. It is almost batlike in its erratic, seesawing flight.

The European Roller does not breed locally but migrates from Europe to spend the summer months in the open woodlands and savannah. Its numbers have declined in many parts of Europe, possibly due to the use of pesticides and a decrease in suitable habitats.

The Redcrested Korhaan may be rather drab but it is distinguished by the robust whistling call of the male during breeding. It stands on a specific site which it uses throughout the season and makes odd tongue-clicking sounds followed by a piercing whistle.

The red crest that gives the Redcrested Korhaan its name is displayed only when the male is courting. For the rest of the time, this bird can be easily overlooked as it uses its plumage and habit of standing still to camouflage itself most effectively.

Bateleurs roost in trees and are sometimes seen sunbathing with their wings spread. They prey on a range of birds, animals and fish – plus carrion, eggs and crustaceans. The young remain dependent on their parents for about 3 to 4 months after their first flight.

Light brown, white-flecked neck plumage and a pale greenish-blue face indicate that this Bateleur is still young. At this time of its life it will spend much of its time scavenging for food. Only as it matures will it begin to take live prey.

Greater Blue-eared Starlings often forage on the ground, equally at home in the bush as in gardens, parks or around restaurant tables.

The male Plumcoloured Starling's iridescent purple plumage makes this bird one of the most colourful in southern Africa, particularly when these birds congregate in flocks. When a raptor is near, a flock of starlings may bunch tightly, so presenting a more intimidating target.

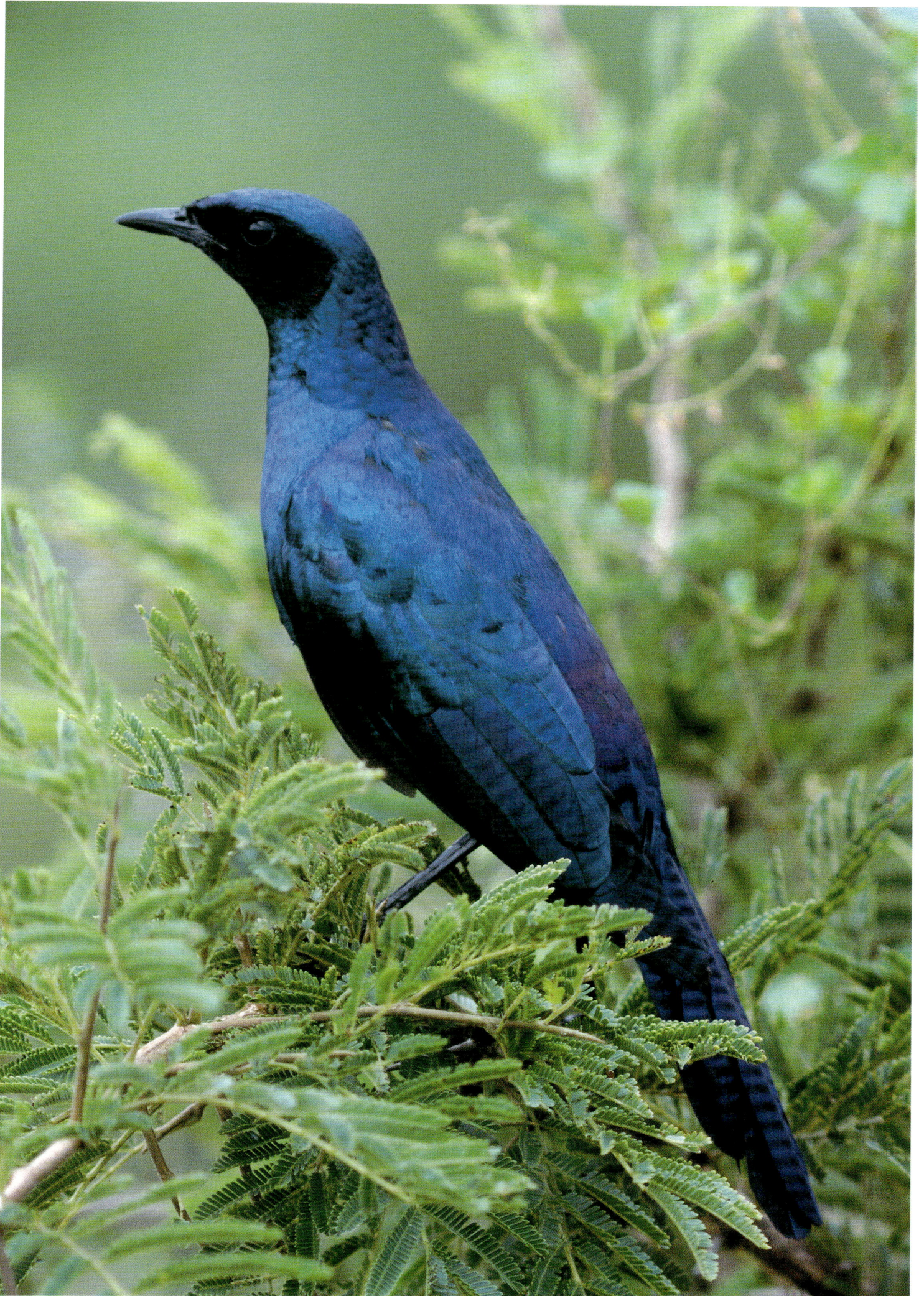

A favourite position for the Burchell's Starling is a perch on top of a tree where this large, noisy bird can advertise its presence with a loud, harsh, high-pitched croaking. These birds prefer trees surrounded by open grass, giving them a better chance of spotting insect prey.

The Dark Chanting Goshawk, named for its melodious chant, builds its stick nest in the fork of a tree. Dung, grass, old rags, hair and the nests of sunbirds may be used to line it. The exterior may be liberally covered with spiders' webs. Generally only a single chick is raised.

DOUBLE-JOINTED FOR DEXTERITY

Like many other raptors, the Gymnogene feeds on prey such as small mammals, reptiles and amphibians. But it is an unusual hawk with an unusual hunting method, for it also clambers about trees and robs birds' nests of their young. It preys on a variety of nestlings, including those of weavers, swallows, swifts and water birds.

Exposed nests are obviously vulnerable, but even those in hollowed tree trunks are not safe. This is because the Gymnogene's legs are uniquely jointed and allow each leg to bend backwards up to 70° and side to side as much as 30°, which enables the birds to extend a leg deep into a hollow and probe for prey.

The normally yellow face of the Gymnogene, whose name means 'bare cheek', turns red when the bird confronts another of its species. It may be a form of display, but some suggest that the 'blush' may be a sign of appeasement when the bird is threatened.

The beautifully coloured Violeteared Waxbill is more common in the drier acacia thornveld where it builds its nest in a shrub or a thorn tree. The oval nests, loosely constructed from dry grass and lined with feathers, are often parasitized by the Shafttailed Whydah.

THE WATER CARRIERS

Whereas the Namaqua Sandgrouse of the desert regions takes water to its young in soaked breast feathers, the diminutive waxbills use a different method.

Several species of these birds fill their crops with food and then drink water. Upon their return to the nest, they are able to feed and water their young in one go.

The attractive little Blue Waxbill becomes quite tame around human habitation, though it will quickly fly into a dense bush if alarmed. The male courts a female by holding a piece of grass in his bill while singing ana bobbing up and down.

The African Scops Owl, here peering out of its nesting hole, is the smallest 'eared' owl in southern Africa. It feeds on insects and scorpions, which, to avoid being stung, it has to attack and incapacitate as quickly as possible.

African Scops Owls roost during the day when the colour and pattern of their feathers makes them virtually invisible as they perch near a tree trunk. Their tufted 'ears' and the dappling effect of leaf shadows help to break up the bird's outline, giving them excellent camouflage.

Whitebacked Vultures, here gathered around an elephant carcass, are typical scavengers. They enjoy a 'feeding association' with many predators, in that the predators do the killing, and the vultures feed on the remains. A carcass may attract hundreds of these birds.

Its long and bare neck enables the Whitebacked Vulture to insert its head deep into a carcass without its plumage being soiled by blood and fluid. The ruff on the shoulders helps prevent the wing feathers from being soiled.

The Southern Carmine Bee-eater is usually a highly gregarious bird, and nests and roosts in groups of hundreds. These birds feed on large flying insects and sometimes congregate around browsing animals to catch insects that have been disturbed by the grazers.

Although feeding here on a harmless butterfly, a Whitefronted Bee-eater can also eat stinging insects without coming to harm. It beats the insect against a branch to stun it and then rubs it against the branch while squeezing it in its bill to expel the venom and the sting.

School of nurture and survival skills for nestlings

Experience gained through trial and error and by following their parents' lead is the way the young of many bird species acquire the skills they need for survival. For many species, it is the only way they can acquire them.

Young ducks and geese learn to follow their mother through a process known as imprinting. Initially they follow any large moving object, but once they have imprinted on their mother, they follow her to the exclusion of anything else. In fact, they then view any other object as a threat and respond by running to their mother for safety.

Through her they gain experience in foraging for food and recognizing threats, to name just two skills.

The young of other birds learn the various calls used by the adults and they also learn to recognize features of their species. Later, when sufficiently mature to begin breeding, they will look for these same features when selecting a mate.

African Paradise Flycatchers, being altricial, hatch naked and blind and are dependent on their parents for food and warmth. Down soon develops, however, protecting the nestlings in cold conditions while the feathers are growing.

Once African Paradise Flycatcher nestlings develop their flight feathers, they spend much of their time perched on the rim of the nest vigorously fluttering their wings, strengthening them in preparation for their first flight, about 11 days after hatching.

Unlike ducks, which leave the nest early, Yellowbilled Egret nestlings remain in the nest until they take their first flight about 35 days after hatching. These shy birds often build their nests in reed beds to conceal them.

KEEPING THE YOUNG SAFE

Luring a potential predator away from their young in the nest, deterring it through swooping close to it or mobbing it, are just some of the ways adult birds ensure the safety of their young.

Ground-nesting Crowned Plovers advance aggressively with wings outspread to drive off an intruder and Indian Mynahs mob the intruder, swooping down on it one after another and calling loudly.

These Barn Owl nestlings display the heart-shaped face so characteristic of the species. The facial plumage directs sound to its ears, the right ear being higher than the left – which enables the owl to locate prey more accurately than if the ears were positioned symmetrically.

Birds of the Kgalagadi ~ 'the great thirst'

The red sands of the Kalahari, carelessly dotted with stunted bushes and camel thorn trees, form the largest area of southern Africa's arid savannah. This acacia-dominated thornveld is bounded in the west by the Namib Desert, in the south by the stony Karoo, in the east by moister bushveld and mixed woodlands, and in the north by the wetlands of the Okavango Delta.

The local name for this forbidding wilderness is *Kgalagadi*, meaning 'the great thirst'. Although it is often assumed to be a desert, this vast stretch of scrubland and fossil valleys, grassy plains and clay pans holds deep subterranean streams. It is this secret water source, as well as the meagre seasonal rains which barely fill the pans, that sustains life in this seemingly barren land.

For a landscape that appears so inhospitable, it is surprisingly rich in bird life. Resident species, consisting mainly of raptors and insect eaters, such as flycatchers, drongos and shrikes, fly over a wide area to exploit patchy food supplies and have erratic breeding cycles to take advantage of the rains. The seasonal birds include seed-eating larks, weavers, sandgrouse and doves. Highly nomadic, they follow the rain in flocks and are constantly on the move to where grasses are seeding.

This bird life is supported by such food as the Kalahari's sparse vegetation offers, and by the many insects, such as beetles, butterflies and millipedes, that are drawn to the seasonal grasses and vegetation.

Bee-eaters have a particular fondness for honeybees and wasps, although they will snatch any flying insect. This bird's elongated bill is ideally suited to catching its stinging prey and holding it at a safe distance from its head. A bee is hijacked from its droning flight and carried back to the bee-eater's perch where it will be slammed against the branch before having its abdomen quickly scraped to remove the sting. Thus disarmed, the bee is swallowed with great relish.

The harvester termite, a common sand dweller, is an easily accessible titbit for birds that prefer to forage on the ground. The Marico Flycatcher often loiters around termite holes, capturing unsuspecting workers as they emerge from their subterranean chambers.

The most conspicuous bird of these scrubby plains is the Ostrich. With its long neck stretching up from its densely feathered body, it stalks haughtily across the burning ground

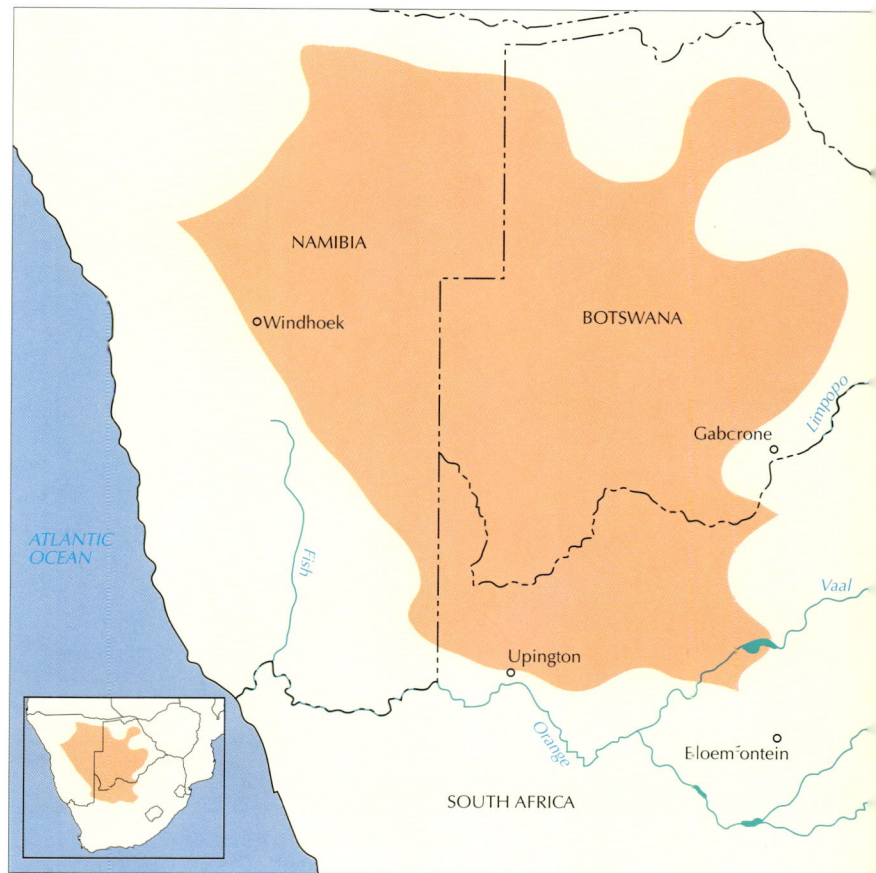

ARID SAVANNAH

A lone Ostrich is an unusual sight, because these birds are sociable and when not breeding live in groups of 35 or so.

The Redeyed Bulbul eats insects, pollen, fruit and nectar, and usually forages in bushes and trees. It also snaps up insects in flight.

Marico Flycatchers perch on a low leafless branch of a tree, ready to fly down to take their insect prey on the ground.

like a large-footed dancer in a tired tutu, its big eyes watchful under outrageously long lashes. The 'camelbird', as it was called in ancient times, is a bird of extraordinary speed, its long legs allowing it to easily outrun enemies and commanding great respect for their mighty kick. It survives on small reptiles and plants, seeds and fruit.

The early hunter-gatherers who once called this land home would wear the skin of this great flightless bird to disguise themselves as they stalked their quarry. Having slain the bird for food, they would raid its nest, empty the bird's large creamy eggshells and use them as 'water bottles'.

The Ostrich was a creature of great importance to these hardy people and often featured in their rock art and folklore. According to one legend, the Mantis, the trickster hero who featured in many of their tales, noticed that a wonderful aroma always accompanied the Ostrich at his mealtimes. Curious, he secretly watched him while he ate and saw that the big bird would furtively draw some glimmering object from beneath his wing and dip his food in it before hurriedly tucking it away again.

Soon afterwards, the wily Mantis invited the Ostrich to a tree that bore delicious yellow plums and tempted him to reach higher and higher into the branches where the ripe fruit hung. Quickly the Mantis snatched the glowing object – an ember – from beneath the bird's upstretched wing and ran away. And that, the tale concludes, is how Mantis brought fire to the people of the plains.

The Ostrich meanwhile, shamed at being so easily tricked, now holds his wings tightly at his sides to protect the remaining precious embers and has never flown since.

The Bateleur, like many raptors of the arid savannah, scours the plains for carrion to supplement its diet of monitor lizards, snakes and small game. This beautiful bird is one of the most magnificent fliers of the African skies. Its name derives from the French word meaning 'tightrope walker', which accurately describes its flight action of rocking from side to side, its wings outstretched as if to steady itself as it 'walks' on the wind.

Unlike the Bateleur, the Whitebacked Vulture is a pure scavenger. It circles the skies slowly, scanning the baked earth for the carcass of an animal that has succumbed to starvation or thirst, or been killed by predators. The remains lie like a bloated offering, the bones already ripped into view by an eager hyena. With a sudden dive, the vulture lands near the carcass, accompanied by scores of fellow scavengers swooping in from seemingly nowhere.

The feeding frenzy that follows is at once awesome and terrible, as the vultures dip their bare necks into the bloody belly of the carcass, unconcerned at the jackal and hyena crowding in alongside them.

Its elaborately forked tail gives the Forktailed Drongo its name. It is a belligerent bird that is quite prepared to attack anything that threatens it – even defending its nest against humans it believes to be intruders.

When disturbed, a Whitefaced Owl indicates its unease by elongating its body and 'eartufts' to look as menacing as possible, while it takes stock of the cause of the disturbance. It is found in dry woodlands, acacia-dominated savannah and bushveld.

A Whitefaced Owl rests while protecting its downy grey-white nestling, which will be ready to leave the nest after about a month. This species often takes over the old nests of raptors, crows and Cape Sparrows.

A BEAK FOR EVERY PURPOSE

The shape of a bird's beak is often a good pointer to its diet and feeding habits. The great hooked beak of the Tawny Eagle is ideally shaped to enable the bird to tear apart the flesh of small animals. In contrast, the Kori Bustard's beak is perfectly suited to foraging, which this bird does by walking slowly and sedately, pecking at insects, seeds and carrion from the ground. Its beak shape also enables the Kori Bustard to feed on the oozing gum of acacia trees – hence its Afrikaans name – *gompou*.

The Tawny Eagle is one of the most versatile raptors. Although it is quite capable of catching its own prey, including birds in flight, it is also a bold and most accomplished pirate of the air. Even the bold Martial Eagle may be robbed of its spoils by this daring thief.

A male Kori Bustard performs its distinctive courtship display, inflating its neck and raising its crest while drooping its wings, its tail raised to fan out the undertail coverts. This display is usually confined to the cooler mornings and evenings of the peak summer months.

Now covered in down, this juvenile Giant Eagle Owl will have grown its flight feathers only after about 3 months. As the largest African owl, it requires a very wide area in which to hunt, so it establishes large territories.

A Giant Eagle Owl sleeps on a branch during the searing heat of the day, saving its hunting exertions for the cooler hours – just after dawn and before dusk.

The Giant Eagle Owl is believed to be one of the few predators, if not the only one, that regularly preys on hedgehogs. It skins the animal first, to remove the spines, before consuming it. Other prey includes birds and a wide variety of small mammals up to the size of hares.

THE LITTLE HAWK

Members of the colourful bee-eater family emulate many of their larger cousins, the raptors, by taking prey on the wing. However, apart from the fact that the bee-eater's prey is of course much smaller (insects as opposed to birds), the method of capture is different from that used by raptors.

Raptors take their prey with their feet, using their talons to grip the bird firmly, whereas the bee-eaters catch their insect prey in their bills.

There are two populations of European Bee-eaters in southern Africa: a local population, breeding in the Western and Northern Cape, and migrants, indistinguishable from the local population, which breed in North Africa, southern Europe and southern Russia.

Swallowtailed Bee-eaters make their nests at the end of metre-long burrows in earth banks. There is some evidence that when leaving the nest, they sometimes close up the entrance with earth, presumably to deter snakes.

THE SANITATION DEPARTMENT

As rich as it is in insects, the savannah is equally rich in wildlife and the carrion eaters play a vital role in clearing up the remains of animals that have died.

Whitebacked Vultures are just one bird species that fulfil this task. Large groups of them gather near kills and ailing wildlife, ready to begin feeding at the first opportunity. Soon, only a few bones will remain, cleanly stripped of flesh.

A flock of Whitebacked Vultures feeds on the carcass of a blue wildebeest, a gathering characterized by fights as every individual looks after itself. The prime aim is to get to the carcass first, so the birds dive at speeds of up to 120 km/h once a feeding opportunity presents itself.

A group of 50 Whitebacked Vultures can strip an impala carcass in about a quarter of an hour. The carcass of an elephant may attract as many as 1 000 birds. The small bare patch at the base of this individual's neck is the crop and will bulge prominently after the bird has fec'.

The discreetly coloured plumage of the female Northern Black Korhaan, with its patterned feathers, provides superb camouflage in the sun-baked grasses of the savannah. It will usually lay only one speckled dark olive-green egg in a slight scrape on the ground.

The conspicuous male Northern Black Korhaan boasts striking plumage. It matches it with an elaborate courting display which involves flying near the female, calling loudly and then slowly descending to the ground on rapidly flapping wings with its yellow legs outstretched.

With one of the biggest beaks for the size of its body, the Southern Yellowbilled Hornbill is an easily identified species. These birds usually forage on the ground for insects and rodents but their huge bill also allows them to eat seeds and fruit. They take refuge in trees if disturbed.

A Southern Yellowbilled Hornbill preens on a branch. Although you cannot see its bill, the small white spots on the primary feathers distinguish it from the Redbilled Hornbill.

A Redbilled Hornbill offers a leaf to its mate in a characteristic display of sociability. These birds live in groups, and if one starts to call, the others soon join in. Their call is a distinctive 'wak, wak, wak' which speeds up into syncopated double notes of 'kawak-kawak-kawak'.

The keen eyesight of a Martial Eagle enables it to spot prey even from heights at which the eagle itself may be invisible from the ground. The attack takes the form of a shallow swooping dive. These birds seldom hover prior to attacking.

ADAPTABILITY IS THE KEY

In common with many raptors, the diet of Martial Eagles ranges from dassies to snakes, leguaans, small buck and a variety of birds – even owls.

They do most of their hunting from the air, using their phenomenal eyesight to locate even the smallest and most expertly camouflaged creature from a great height.

Young Martial Eagles are less adept at hunting the birds that will form a large part of their diet when they are adults, so they often prey instead on domestic chickens, which are far easier to catch and more visible. For this reason, Martial Eagles have tended to be harassed and this, combined with their slow reproduction rate, is leading to reduced numbers of these magnificent birds.

A Martial Eagle crouches over a recently captured leguaan to conceal it from any other raptor that may attempt to take it. Leguaans make up the largest part of the diet of Martial Eagles in the northern part of southern Africa.

The incubation of Ostrich eggs takes between 39 and 53 days. They are laid about 48 hours apart, in the afternoon or evening.

These two female Ostriches and their mate may produce about 40 eggs in a breeding season, the length of which may depend on rainfall in more arid regions. The chicks leave the nest, a 3 m scrape in sandy ground, immediately after hatching.

THE REMARKABLE RATITES

Ostriches belong to a group of flightless birds called the ratites, which includes the Rheas of South America, the Emus and Cassowaries of Australia and the Kiwis of New Zealand.

The Ostrich thrives in a dangerous environment in which enemies may include the large carnivores. With its speed, large-toed feet and method of attack – a powerful downward-raking kick – the Ostrich is a formidable foe. It can severely injure even a fully grown lion.

Ostriches are quite capable of running at speeds of up to 60 km/h for as much as a kilometre. During the breeding season, males become very aggressive and are formidable adversaries, with a height of 2 m and a mass of over 100 kg.

Lizards make up about half of the diet of Pygmy Falcons, with insects making up the balance. These striking little birds use the nest chambers of Sociable Weavers to breed, and studies suggest that the weavers derive some protection from the falcons.

Pale Chanting Goshawks hunt mainly from a perch, swooping down on prey and even chasing it after landing if they have to. They also walk about hunting for reptiles, insects, small mammals and carrion. The brown markings show that this specimen is a young bird.

KEEPING PESTS IN CHECK

The value of owls to agriculture is undisputed as these birds feed on a wide range of potentially damaging species such as mice, large populations of which can do immense damage to crops. Owls also eat insects – some of which pose the same danger to agriculture if unchecked.

The Barn Owl is found on every continent, except Antarctica, and on many islands. It has also been introduced to some islands to combat rats and mice.

In the Seychelles, for example, they were introduced for this purpose, but they have now become a pest in their own right. These owls reduced the rodent population to such an extent that they now prey on Fairy Terns and have probably caused a reduction in the population of the endemic Seychelles Kestrel because of competition for nest sites. This is an exception, however. Generally, this family of birds is valuable in helping to keep populations of potentially damaging species under control.

The Barn Owl is one of nature's most efficient predators of small mammals and large insects. These birds begin to hunt at dusk and use their acute sense of hearing to locate prey, though on moonlit nights their excellent eyesight also plays an important role in the hunt.

Spotted Eagle Owls roost on the ground or in a tree during the day and hunt nocturnally for insects, birds, mammals, reptiles, frogs and, occasionally, fish. Their biggest threat is probably the motor car – these birds are often killed at night by road traffic.

Adult Bateleurs feed on just about anything that walks, flies or has died. They hunt live prey by swooping on it or gently parachuting down on it, by holding their wings up, extending their legs and taking the prey in their powerful feet armed with razor-sharp talons.

A young Bateleur will attain full adult plumage only after about 7 or 8 years – if it survives that long. The practice of laying poisoned bait has resulted in the decline of these magnificent birds and they are now found in only a fraction of their former range.

The bustle of bathing, cleaning and preening

All birds bathe. This somewhat involved activity is vital, since dirty feathers stick together and do not insulate the birds properly, nor do they streamline the head and body, thus hindering flight. Fishing birds, such as the cormorant, which feed on fast-moving fish by catching them underwater, must be streamlined for swimming as well as flight if they are to be able to hunt successfully.

Bathing is an instinctive action – even a fledgling may perform bathing movements when exposed to water for the first time, a small bowlful being quite sufficient to trigger the action. Surprisingly, water birds bathe too, upending themselves first on their heads and then balancing on their tails in even the deepest water.

Large land birds bathe in the shallows, where they are still able to stand. Smaller birds use puddles, quickly dipping their heads below the surface, then standing erect so that water droplets race down their back and tail.

Then they ruffle their body plumage, crouch in the water and flap their wings, spattering the surface of the puddle with a spray of water droplets. Again and again they dip their heads and flap their wings, until their plumage is partially wetted. The vigorous flapping cleans the feathers, dislodging parasites, flakes of skin and feather debris prior to preening – which is easier if the plumage is wetted.

An Egyptian Goose flaps energetically during its bathing routine to dislodge particles of dirt and wet its plumage prior to preening.

The Whitefaced Duck has been known to dive under the surface to feed on aquatic plants and animals but it usually forages in mud for food. This stains its face brown, so thorough bathing is required to ensure recognition: courtship involves the pair facing one another.

The plumage on top of a Swift Tern's head is a cap of feathers, slicked back during bathing and preening. This streamlines the head and neck for flight and for its plunge into the sea in pursuit of its prey.

THE IMPORTANCE OF PREENING

After bathing, all birds preen themselves as the extra weight of the water makes flight more difficult, thus making the bird more vulnerable to predators. First, however, some birds, such as ducks, dry their plumage by flapping their wings and shaking their bodies while their feathers are still ruffled.

They then rub their heads and necks against their bodies or a firm surface such as a branch to press excess water from these areas. They pull each long feather through their bills to squeeze out any water flapping failed to shed. Scratching with their feet also helps the drying process.

Some species take a dust bath before preening. Larks and pigeons, for instance, bathe in dry dust by using their beaks and feet to scratch out a shallow saucer-shaped depression in dry earth. Then they ruffle their plumage to allow the dust to penetrate it and cover the feathers. Many species do this by kicking up clouds of dust with their feet. All species end this type of bath the same way – with a

A Water Dikkop dries its wings by beating them so rapidly on the surface that they become a blur. After excess water has been removed, the feathers will be preened neatly back into place. This species prefers to run rather than fly when disturbed.

vigorous shake of the body while the feathers are still ruffled. Some species, such as pigeons, bathe in both water or dust.

To preen itself, a bird rubs its bill over the preen gland at the base of its tail, releasing the preen oil and spreading it over its plumage, especially its flight feathers. It is thought that the oil helps to condition the feathers, which are also smoothed and arranged during preening. The bill is the most important tool, but many species also use their feet to preen. Another bird, of the same species, may preen inaccessible areas, such as the head. This is called allopreening.

Spottedbacked Weavers bathe every day and are usually found near water – in savannahs and also in urban areas, where birdbaths are sure to be found. Fast-flying flocks of these gregarious birds quickly take over a puddle or birdbath for a communal bathing session.

Burning skies and sheltering wings

A story goes that, in ancient times, God spent many long days tenderly shaping the forests and mountains, kloofs and valleys of Africa. When He was done, He stood up and clapped His hands in delight at the beauty of His creation – great clouds of dust billowed from His hands and settled heavily onto the place where He had been sitting, and this became the Karoo.

Dominating the central plateau, the Karoo is the semi-arid part of southern Africa's desert lands, merging in the east with the highveld grasslands and fading westward into the Namib, southern Africa's only true desert, which stretches along the western coastline from the Kunene River in the north to the Orange River in the south. It is a desolate landscape of surreal beauty and of startling contrasts, from the sensual shiftings of sand dunes to that spectacular wound gouged into the earth, the Fish River Canyon, and from a rare and grudging rainfall to a nightly fog that steals in off the cold Benguela Current, smothering the barren coastal stretch in a blanket of icy moisture.

This pitiless land, where water is often just a cruel mirage spilling shimmering pools across the earth, is a world where birds survive in sheer defiance of drought, erratic food supply and searing heat.

One intrepid desert survivor is the mottled brown Namaqua Sandgrouse. At dawn, when the day is still cool, large flocks of these birds set off and head for a water hole that may be as far as 80 km away. As they arrive at their favoured drinking spot, sometimes in their thousands, they cautiously circle for a while, to check for predators. Then they land to drink quickly. While doing so, however, the male soaks his breast feathers in the water. Then he returns to his waiting young who eagerly quench their thirst by sipping from the waterlogged feathers.

Like many desert birds, Rüppell's Korhaan spends much of its time on the ground, scratching among the stones for insects and seeds. It is therefore shrewdly camouflaged to hide it from predators. These Namib wanderers are notoriously difficult to spot. Their flightless young are also so cleverly marked that when a chick lies still with its neck outstretched – an instinctive response when threatened – it virtually disappears into the gravelly background by closely resembling a rock or piece of wood. This habit of freezing when danger is sensed is crucial for survival in a vast, isolated habitat where threadbare vegetation offers little refuge from circling raptors.

Namaqua Sandgrouse can go for 3 to 5 days without drinking, but many small desert birds are able to avoid dehydration by relying almost totally on moisture from insects, fruit and unripe grass seeds. Active on the edge of day, when the sun is low and the air cool, they forage and

DESERTS AND SEMIDESERTS

The plumage of a Rüppell's Korhaan so closely matches the colour of its domain that it is difficult to see even on open desert plains.

scramble for food. But when noon's glare brings a dense breathlessness to the landscape, the birds become still, huddling silently in the slightest shade, fiercely intent on conserving energy and maintaining a body temperature that will keep them alive.

The brutal heat is particularly dangerous for fledglings. For instance, Sclater's Lark, endemic to the rocky Karoo, builds its nest among stones and pebbles with little or no cover and lays a single egg in a small, cup-shaped indentation in the ground. The newly hatched nestling is very vulnerable and is solicitously cared for by both parents, who take turns to stand over the nest and shade the young bird, for leaving it exposed to full sun would condemn it to certain death. While one parent is so engaged, the other forages for termites to feed it.

The desert is a forbidding place, requiring a life of discipline and absolute attention to the availability of water, food supplies and the lethal shifts in temperature. It is a place where life is constantly stalked by death, where a sudden shadow falling across a lethargic Spotted Dikkop could signal a water-laden Namaqua Sandgrouse returning to its young – or a Peregrine Falcon swooping down to attack.

The Bokmakierie is the exception to the rest of its family of secretive and retiring bush shrikes. It is often seen out in the open, advertising its territory through a repertoire of calls.

Although associated with the desert regions, the Namaqua Dove wanders widely across Africa, visiting grassy plains and moister woodlands. It is camouflaged equally well among lichen-encrusted branches or on barren, stony soil.

The Doublebanded Courser lays its single egg in the open, trusting that cryptic markings will help the egg merge into the surroundings.

Doublebanded Coursers nest on bare open spaces which give them a good view of the surrounding area and early warning of any danger. Their preferred prey is harvester termites, which they peck from the ground after a brief darting run.

The breast feathers of the male Namaqua Sandgrouse are adapted to absorb water and are used to carry the vital liquid back to his young. Every day as dawn breaks, flocks of these fascinating birds fly to water holes as far as 80 km from the nest, to drink and collect water.

The nomadic Redheaded Finch has a peculiar habit of taking over the deserted nests of other birds, carefully relining them to its own taste before moving in.

The male Redheaded Finch is distinguished by its fiery flush, while the plainer female keeps a cooler head. These small birds often travel in mixed flocks with other seed eaters like canaries and waxbills, gathering at water holes in dense fluttering clouds.

The adaptable Yellow Canary is one of those species able to thrive in a range of habitats. Equally at home in domestic gardens, fynbos, montane shrub and grassland, it is also found in arid regions. Seeds and insects make up a large part of its diet.

Greater Kestrels, often found in arid areas, usually perch on vantage points such as termite mounds or trees and catch lizards, rodents and insects by swooping down on them, but they can also take small birds in flight. This is a juvenile as it has dark eyes and a brown-barred tail.

DUEL IN THE SUN

In arid lands, where food is scarce and small birds and mammals are artfully skilled at concealment, patience and opportunistic vigilance is honed to a fine art by raptors.

Constantly, hunter and hunted stage a deadly contest against the stark desert backdrop. Raptors launch lightning attacks on birds gathered to drink. Their prey relies on the many eyes of the flock to spot an impending assault, and the confusion created by their large numbers to foil it.

Because of its pale eyes, the Greater Kestrel is also known as the White-eyed Kestrel. This desert hunter displays surprisingly frugal habits, recycling disused crows' nests for its own use and hoarding food under stones or among grass tufts.

THE POSTURING MASTER OF CAMOUFLAGE

Spotted Dikkops favour stony arid areas with some scrub, where their eggs and nests – shallow scrapes surrounded by haphazard arrangements of pebbles, droppings and plant debris – are almost invisible.

Wonderfully camouflaged in their speckled plumage, they negate much of this benefit by being highly territorial, loud and noisy. Males run at intruders with their heads low against the ground and wings spread. These birds are also most vocal at night and on overcast days, particularly after it has rained.

One of the best features of the Spotted Dikkop is its pair of beautifully accentuated yellow eyes. Their size allows it to feed at night and during the low-light periods of twilight and dawn. This bird feeds on insects, frogs and small reptiles, snatching them up in its long bill.

While shading eggs from the blistering heat, a Spotted Dikkop will lift its feathers for ventilation. Panting also has a slight cooling effect.

Large yellow eyes provide the only bright splash of colour in the Spotted Dikkop's highly effective camouflage as it nests in open scrub. It is lethargic and quiet on cloudless days, saving its energy and loud piping song for nocturnal activities and overcast days.

FLAMBOYANCE IN A BARREN LAND

The sight of a flock of Rosyfaced Lovebirds screeching and whistling as they race at breakneck speed in a tight knot of greens and pinks across the barren rocks of Namibia is a breathtaking display of incongruity.

These brightly coloured 'bag ladies' of the air, with their curious habit of transporting nest material in their rump feathers, bring a note of surrealism to the tawny landscape, challenging assumptions about the colours of birds that inhabit arid zones.

Many people associate members of the parrot family with lush forests. The Rosyfaced Lovebird, however, is found on scrubby hillsides and in rocky terrain, including river canyons, in arid areas of the Northern Cape Province, Namibia and southwestern Angola.

They nest in crevices and holes or in the abandoned nests of Sociable Weavers and are strictly monogamous: they bond with their mates while still immature and maintain their partnerships for life.

A noisy flock of Rosyfaced Lovebirds is a visual treat. Flocks range in size from only a few birds to many hundreds at a good source of food. They have a varied appetite and will feed on seeds, grain, fruit, flowers and even nectar – whatever is abundant and accessible.

Although argumentative and aggressive, the Rosyfaced Lovebird is transformed when courting, becoming intimately engrossed in mutual preening. When building a nest, it stuffs straw and twigs into its rump feathers with its beak to transport the material to the chosen site.

A flock of Redbilled Queleas in a thorn tree is a sight to strike fear into a farmer's heart. Over 1 billion in number, these birds are the world's most common and are akin to locusts in the damage they can do to crops. Roosting flocks may contain several million individuals.

Birds of a feather wheeling and swooping as one

Cape Cormorant nursery colonies may contain 40 000 nests. These are not the largest assemblies, however, as several sea birds breed in colonies of a million or more.

In South Africa, the Cape Cormorant is the only marine cormorant which regularly forages in large flocks, sometimes containing thousands of individuals. These gregarious birds feed on shoaling fish such as pilchards; individuals settle on the surface and then dive for their prey.

THE UNSOLVED MYSTERY

A huge flock of thousands of queleas twists and turns in a stunning aerial ballet, each bird wheeling and swooping as if tied to its neighbours.

How so many birds can manoeuvre so rapidly without colliding is one of the unsolved mysteries of nature. Equally puzzling is how a huge group of birds will suddenly take to the air as one. Perhaps so-called 'intention movements' trigger each action: a bird flexes its legs to take off and its neighbours instantly follow suit, or a bird in the air notes the intention of the leading birds to alter course – and follows.

Crested Francolins roost in trees at night and often huddle together for warmth and mutual protection.

A colony of Southern Carmine Bee-eaters may number as many as 2 000 individuals, which riddle a steep bank with nesting burrows each about 1 m deep. They dig with their beaks, leaning on their wings to sweep dirt out with their feet. Each burrow ends in a nesting chamber.

Every night Little Bee-eaters return to the same perch and huddle together for warmth. Grouped like this they are more likely to spot predators and can warn each other of danger. During the day, however, they disperse and hunt alone for insects.

SECURITY IN NUMBERS

Why do birds form flocks and colonies? Why are some birds, such as Cape Gannets, found only in flocks and colonies, while other species, such as Cape Turtle Doves, seem to be equally happy on their own, or with a partner, or in flocks sometimes numbering hundreds?

Sometimes birds breed colonially because they have to: there are large areas over which they have to forage but very limited breeding space, on islands for instance.

But there are many benefits in forming flocks and colonies. It is more difficult for intruders to approach unnoticed and even those far larger than an individual bird can be intimidated by an aggressive display from a group of many birds.

In an amazing example of the benefits of forming flocks, pelicans seek their prey as a group. An armada of pelicans feeds by herding a hapless shoal of fish into the shallows where they can be picked off with ease.

Pelicans hunt as well as fly in a flock, forming a living 'net' by surrounding a shoal of fish before feeding on it. Their huge pouches and long bills enable them to catch many fish at once – but they do not store their catch in the pouch, as is commonly believed.

Large flocks of Cape Gannets follow the 'sardine run' up the east coast every year. Each bird eats about 300g of fish a day.

A shortage of suitable, predator-free islands off the South African coast is a major reason for colonial breeding on the part of Cape Gannets. Some authorities state that only 6 islands are used by these birds – evidence of the limited availability of breeding space for the species.

Cape Turtle Doves are found on their own, in pairs, or in flocks of thousands. Flocking is particularly obvious in arid regions. Raptors wait at water holes so that they can take prey coming to drink, but flocking provides safety in numbers by reducing risk to an individual.

From a distance a flock of Lesser Flamingos forms a pink cloud; when settled on a pan it gives the impression of a soft pink mat. These magnificent birds feed on blue-green algae living in fresh water, filtering the organisms through their specialized bills with their tongues.

SAFETY IN THE AIR

Avoiding each other in the air is a skill at which birds are adept, but there is another aspect to the coordinated movements of a flock in flight. Starlings, for example, fly in tight groups, erratically veering this way and that, which confuses predators such as falcons. In the flurry of wings they are unable to single out their quarry and may also face the danger of colliding with other birds in the flock. Deterred, the predators turn away to seek easier prey.

Sanderlings resemble clockwork toys as they speed about foraging for food, dashing back and forth across a beach following the surge of the sea. They migrate great distances – those found in South Africa coming from breeding grounds in north-central Siberia.

Lightning birds that follow the rain

Pula, the currency of Botswana, is also the Setswana word for 'rain' and is used as a hearty greeting that carries in it a blessing and a wish for fulfilment. This use of the word reveals a profound understanding that the true wealth of Africa, the real currency of a dry land, is water.

The rain that falls on southern Africa flows from the continental divide in dongas and spruits that begin like fine veins on the high plateau, then grow and widen into great river systems across the land, and finally drain into the sea.

The range of aquatic habitats in southern Africa is wide and varied, ranging from brackish saltpans in the interior to river mouths and low-lying marshy areas on the coast, rocky streams to deep muddy rivers, and dams to swampy vleis. The features of some of these habitats change with the seasons, as flood is followed by drought, dramatically transforming the vegetation and landscape.

Many water birds have an uncanny ability to follow the rain and will begin arriving at newly flooded saltpans – in the Kalahari, for example – from hundreds of kilometres away. Among them are flamingos, sometimes numbering hundreds of thousands and forming a breathtaking sight as they wing their rosy way across the desert skies towards a shimmering pan. The flamingo is named *nonyane ya tladi* in Setswana – the lightning bird – perhaps because these birds often congregate on the pans after heavy thunderstorms.

Specializing in the minute blue-green algae that grow in the salty water, Lesser Flamingos hang their heads into the shallow waters and filter the algae from the briny water with their unique bills.

The African Jacana is another true water bird, but one that prefers the fresh water of the tropical wetlands, marshes and lagoons where there is plenty of floating vegetation. Stalking daintily across lily pads on long splayed feet, a male African Jacana may appear to be carrying a small bundle of twigs beneath each wing.

As he reaches the bank he unceremoniously deposits two small chicks on the mossy rock where they stand perplexed but safe on spidery toes. The male, with a harem of up to 4 mates, assumes full parental responsibility for his offspring from the time the eggs are laid. The young live on a variety of insects and larvae that they pick from the floating vegetation.

Besides leguaans and otters, which share their habitat and regard them as prey, young jacanas are vulnerable to the brightly coloured but brutish Purple Gallinule. Snorting as it scrambles across a mat of bent reeds, it plunders any nest that it comes across, removing and eating the eggs and nestlings with great relish and very little delicacy.

The more stately and dignified Goliath Heron will only eat fish, wading out into the water until it is at belly-level to

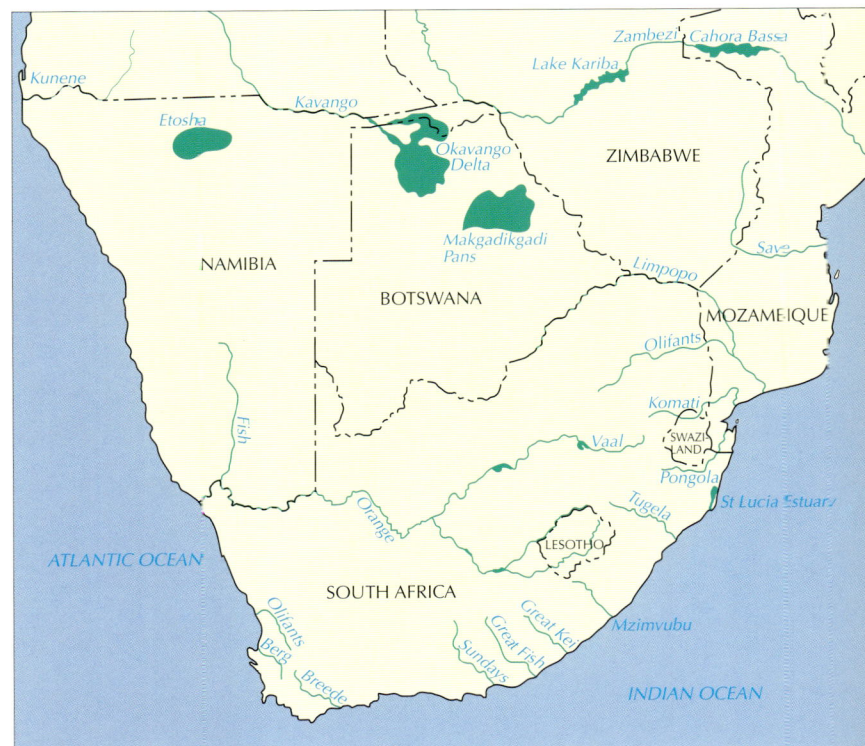

A Saddlebilled Stork flies solo across the vast Okavango floodplains in Botswana.

WETLANDS

The bubbling song of the Burchell's Coucal is so closely associated with wet weather that it has led to the bird being dubbed the Rainbird.

do its hunting. With a sudden lunge it spears a fish with its long sharp beak and carries it back to the bank to eat it.

An African Fish Eagle that has been watching the heron from its waterside perch with detached interest, now becomes intent on the fish wriggling furiously in the heron's bill. With two downy white eaglets ravenously waiting in its high nest of sticks and leaves, the parent has to step up its hunting to keep them satisfied. With astonishing speed the great whiteheaded bird is suddenly upon the heron, and in a confusion of wide flapping wings and grasping talons, the fish is snatched and the poacher is gone with a high-pitched cry of triumph.

Besides being a rich and consistent source of food, the soft sand banks, rank weeds and vegetation that flourish along waterways and on the edges of marshes and lakes provide great opportunities for nest building – both as sites and as a source of material for nests.

The Malachite Kingfisher burrows holes into the banks along waterways, while mixed colonies of Reed Cormorants, African Darters and herons build platforms of reeds and sticks in reed beds, bushes or trees, usually over water.

The brilliantly coloured male Red Bishop builds a number of nests in reed beds, weaving them out of strips of grass and reeds and skilfully attaching them to the reed stems. It may acquire up to 7 mates in a season, each of which will carefully examine and select a nest before mating. When the female is incubating, the male makes no further parental contribution except to defend the colony from predators such as lizards and rats.

The huge nest of the Hamerkop is a remarkable structure of sticks, reeds and any debris that the bird chances upon. Sometimes the enormous oven-shaped dwelling is built with the co-operation of 4 or more birds. Mud is smoothly plastered over it as more material is added. It often takes some months to complete the nest which may have a roof up to a metre thick.

Sadly, it is not unusual for the patiently engineered nest to be taken over by Barn Owls or even bees, and it seems to be irresistible to ducks which often breed on the broad roof.

The dark and sinister-looking Hamerkop has long been regarded with awe and superstition among indigenous people. According to San legend, this bird is able to see the future reflected in water, often the image of someone over whom the shadow of death hangs. And it helpfully warns the person who is due to die by flying over their shelter and calling plaintively.

The Hamerkop, named for the shape of its head and renowned for its enormous nest, feeds mainly on frogs.

A Little Egret shuffles a foot in the murky water to stir the sandy bottom and disturb small crustaceans and fish. This is an energetic hunter that searches the waters with much head darting and quick flapping runs.

FEATHERED RIBBONS IN FASHION

The ivory plumes of the Little Egret trail and lift in the wind like satin streamers. These elegant feathers are an integral element in its elaborate courtship display and may also be used in shows of aggression.

The decorative quality of the egret's beautiful breeding plumage did not escape the attention of the fashion-conscious at the turn of the century, when this small white heron all but disappeared in parts of its range as it was enthusiastically hunted down. The 'aigrettes' were used as head adornments, or decorations for women's hats.

Although there remains some interest in the plumes of the Little Egret, mainly from the Far East, there is no longer any threat to its widespread population.

Although the Little Egret prefers to feed alone, it will gather in hundreds at a rich food source. It breeds in large colonies with other egrets and herons, its nest, a platform of twigs – set somewhat higher than those of the smaller birds – in a reed bed or a tree.

The unmistakable African Fish Eagle bears itself with great dignity, whether in flight or at rest. It spends hours perched on a bare branch overlooking water, simply observing the surroundings or preening itself – little more than 8 minutes a day is spent actually fishing.

The African Fish Eagle rarely hunts while soaring, preferring to drop down from its post to catch its quarry in its large talons. The soles of its feet are roughened with tiny spines to prevent slippery fish from escaping its grasp. This stately hunter also preys on baby crocodiles.

BEAUTIFUL BUT SLOVENLY HOUSEKEEPERS

Despite their name, kingfishers are not all associated with water, neither are they all fishing birds. Some species are confined to woodland and thrive on insects, spiders and worms, not eating fish at all, or only rarely.

The handsome Malachite Kingfisher, however, is one of the family that does take fish. It forms a lifetime bond with its mate and usually nests in a hole in a riverbank. Both sexes engage in the excavation of the tunnel which they place high enough to escape the attention of predators.

Kingfishers are not noted for the cleanliness of their burrows which can become fouled by excreta and littered with fish bones and the remains of regurgitated meals. Even though the Malachite Kingfisher builds its tunnel at a slope to allow for some drainage, sanitation remains a problem. After tending their young, the parents often need to clean themselves by diving repeatedly into water.

Unlike most aquatic kingfishers which hunt primarily by diving from waterside perches, the Pied Kingfisher is more inclined to hover. It hangs for a moment in the air, catches sight of its prey, takes aim and then plunges headfirst into the water to seize the fish.

So tiny that the most slender stem will carry its weight, the Malachite Kingfisher will often bob its head and body up and down in the reeds while it watches for movement in the water. Despite its bright colours it may escape notice until it suddenly flies from its low perch.

A flock of Greater Flamingos moves in an enormous honking mass across the shallow Sowa Pan in Botswana. This is the larger of the two species of flamingo found in Africa. It sifts crustaceans, molluscs and diatoms from mud, which it forces through bristles in its bill.

Perfectly poised on one slender leg this Greater Flamingo preens itself with its heavy pink bill. Its amazingly mobile neck is the longest, proportionately, among southern African birds.

The Lesser Flamingo is an extremely specialized feeder, in that its bill is designed to filter and extract blue-green algae and diatoms from brackish water. It often feeds at night, hanging its head over the moonlit water and swinging its bill rhythmically from side to side.

A Purple Gallinule highsteps through a marshy vlei on gawky red legs, preferring to clamber heavily through the reeds rather than fly. It is widespread in the swampy wetlands of southern Africa. It may hold its food, which includes plants and nestlings, in its foot while eating.

The African Jacana, often called the Lily-trotter, picks its way daintily across a carpet of water lilies. If it slows down it will sink a little before it sets off again. Females are heavier than males and are more restricted in the type of vegetation across which they can forage.

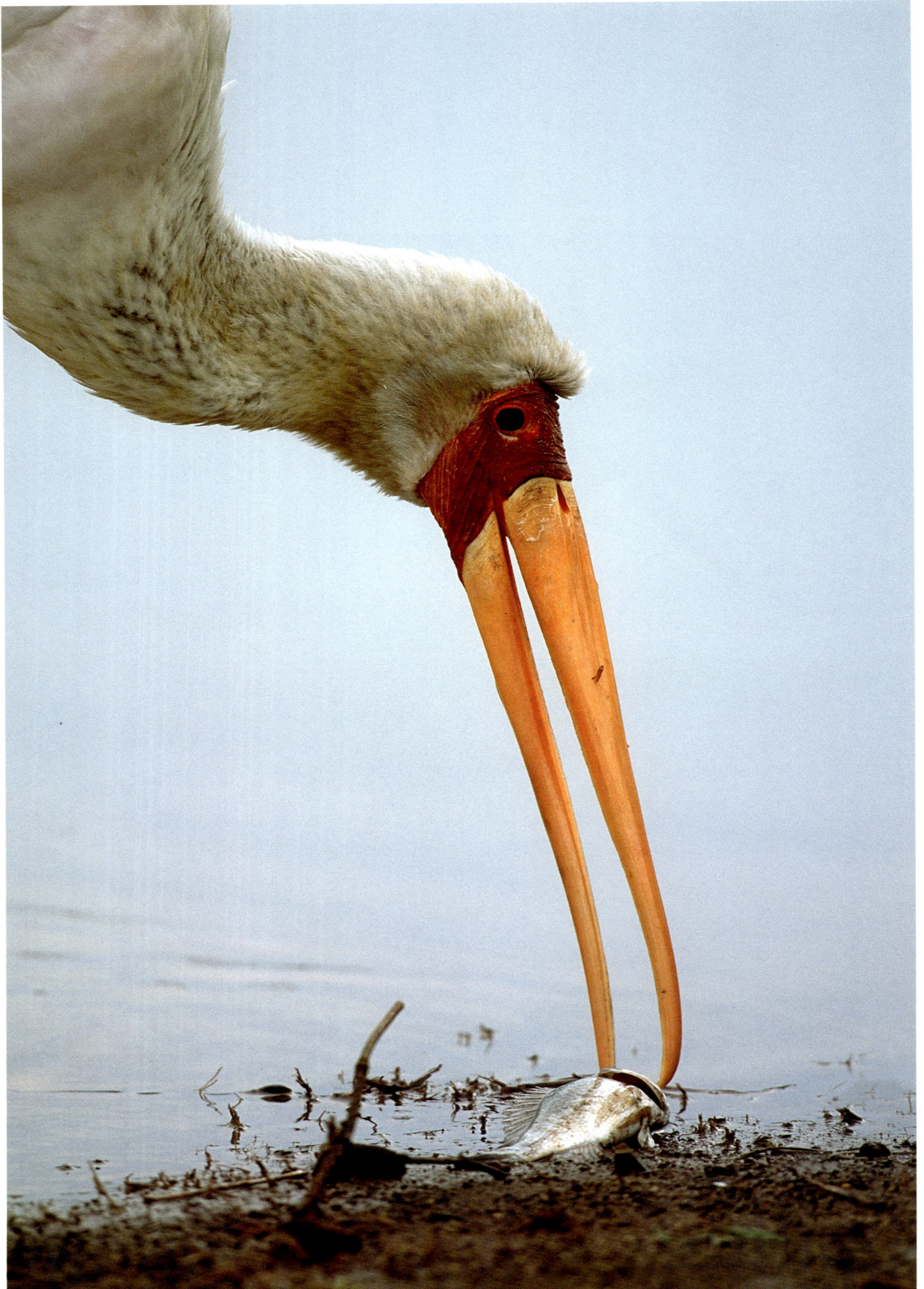

The Yellowbilled Stork has an unusual way of expressing alarm, suddenly freezing and lowering its beak as it stares anxiously ahead. This sudden stillness creates a ripple effect among neighbouring storks as they also become motionless, forming a hushed tableau.

With a delicate arch of its wing this Yellowbilled Stork creates a shadow to entice fish closer. It feeds its nestlings by regurgitating food into the nest, a bulky platform of sticks and straw built in a tree. Nestlings may also be cooled by the parent regurgitating water over them.

During breeding, the plumage of the adult Yellowbilled Stork deepens in hue, a rosy pink bringing a characteristic blush to the white feathers.

The Egyptian Goose, immortalized in paintings in the Pharaohs' tombs, stretches its wings back during a courtship dance. After breeding, a pair will maintain their partnership for life. This is one of the most widespread ducks in Africa.

The Fulvous Duck is closely related to swans and has the same long trachea through which it produces its high, wheezing whistle. It feeds primarily on aquatic seeds and fruit, dabbling for food but also using its very large feet to dive below the surface when necessary.

A Sacred Ibis stands perfectly mirrored in the placid waters. Because of its sooty head and neck, which are bare of feathers, it is called the skoorsteenveër *(chimney sweep) in Afrikaans. Both a scavenger and predator, it feeds on a variety of food including offal and carrion.*

BIRD OF ANCIENT MYTH AND LEGEND

Ironically, the Sacred Ibis is extinct in the very land that gave it its name. The ancient Egyptians venerated the bird as the incarnation of Thoth, the moon god and scribe who officiated in the judgment of the dead and who was often depicted with the head of the ibis.

The appearance of this extraordinary looking bird along the banks of the Nile after a flood was believed to be a sign that a good harvest was coming. As with other creatures featured in Egyptian temples and regarded with reverence, the Sacred Ibis was often mummified and placed in tombs.

In southern Africa this bird is very widespread, frequenting vleis, floodplains and estuaries and often seen flying in a silent, undulating line.

Ibises are closely related to storks, with which they share the ability to detect food in the water more by touch than by sight. This graceful Glossy Ibis wades slowly through shallow water, feeling and probing for food such as crustaceans, molluscs and fish.

The Blacksmith Plover places its eggs in an exposed scrape in the sandy shores of dams, vleis or pans. It will agitatedly attack anyone walking too close to its nest site, its voice rising in a shrieking, clinking sound that resembles a hammer hitting an anvil.

FRESH WATER OR SALT WATER?

The Blacksmith Plover, the most familiar member of the plover family in southern Africa, is mainly a creature of fresh-water shores, where it pecks at easily accessible worms and molluscs that wriggle in waterlogged sand. It also feeds on dry land, consuming a variety of insects, especially beetles, crickets and caterpillars.

The Pied Avocet, with its long legs and bill, is a wader and frequents saltpans, sewage works and tidal lagoons. It forages in shallow waters, sweeping its black upcurved bill from side to side across the surface of the water.

From time to time it submerges its entire head and nudges the muddy bottom for crustaceans or any detritus that it can scoop up. It also feeds while swimming, upending itself like a duck to take prey underwater.

The red eyes of this Pied Avocet distinguish it from the female, which has brown eyes. This bird swallows large numbers of small stones which accumulate in the stomach and help it grind up its hard-shelled crustacean prey.

Largely nocturnal, a Pel's Fishing Owl emerges from its shady roosting site to hunt at dusk. Its long talons and the spiny undersides of its toes and feet enable this bird to get a good grip on its slippery prey.

Highly gregarious, large colonies of Red Bishops breed in reed beds where they pack their tightly woven nests into small areas. The male develops its bold red plumage during breeding but otherwise resembles the plainer female with its streaky brown colouring.

The swollen knobs on the head of this Redknobbed Coot may resemble wounds but are, in fact, indicators that the bird is in breeding condition. These aggressive and territorial birds are a common sight on lakes and dams throughout southern Africa.

THE FINE ART OF SEDUCTION

Many birds of the waterways have the most innovative ways of expressing their willingness to begin breeding. The plumage of the male often becomes suffused with colour which he may display in an enchanting dance of seduction.

The Red Bishop becomes transformed from a drab little bird into a fiery suitor in splendid red livery, leaping and fluttering among reed beds to attract a female, while the Little Egret dons ribbon-like alabaster plumes, which he elegantly lifts and fans in a visually entrancing ballet.

The Knobbilled Duck, however, like the Redknobbed Coot, relies on the enlargement of an anatomical feature to draw attention to himself. By edging sideways towards the female with his neck bowed and much tail flicking and feather raising, he tries to impress the female by showing off the size of the distinctive black comb on his upper mandible.

The male Knobbilled Duck displays a black comb on its bill which becomes more pronounced during the breeding season. Even the feeding habits of these birds are sexually defined, the males stripping grass of seeds while the females dabble in the shallows.

Although the most common of freshwater cormorants, the Reed Cormorant is not seen in large numbers. It prefers to feed alone and may sit for long periods on a rock or bare stump on the water's edge. It is named for its tendency to roost among reeds but it will also roost in trees.

An African Darter suns itself after a fishing trip, spreading its waterlogged feathers out to dry. A fine swimmer, it propels itself smoothly through the water with only its long thin neck and head showing. Because of this peculiar swimming style it is also called the Snakebird.

A flock of Eastern White Pelicans forms an elaborate signature in the sky over Lake St Lucia in KwaZulu-Natal, where they breed in the winter months.

Graceful and effortless in flight, an Eastern White Pelican becomes cumbersome and ungainly on the ground, or as it lands, skidding into the water with a great splash.

Pelicans are extremely intolerant of disturbance while breeding and require a secure and inaccessible site. Hence, there are only a few breeding colonies in southern Africa. These Eastern White Pelicans are classified as rare, as are their Pinkbacked cousins.

ADVERTISING FOR PARTNERS

Despite appearing to be a solitary, unsociable bird, the Grey Heron is not averse to company and will readily nest in colonies. This is more likely in the southern parts of its range where it may take over an old nest in a heronry that is also home to a number of other species, including egrets, darters and freshwater cormorants.

After selecting a nest – an untidy platform of sticks and twigs in a tree or reed bed – it indicates its readiness for a mate. The heron publicizes itself with a series of ritualistic jabbing and bowing movements, with its crest raised and plumes splayed. From its nest it points its reddened beak to the sky, slowly lowering its body into a tight crouch and making loud yelping sounds. This display continues until it is chosen by a female.

Grey Herons stand arrayed like desert sentinels as they rest on the lip of a vast undulating sand dune near Sandwich Harbour in Namibia. Besides aquatic creatures, which they hunt by wading in shallow water, they will also kill reptiles, small mammals and birds.

A Grey Heron may stalk along the water's edge, actively fishing, or may simply stand for long periods, waiting for something edible to swim by. Should a fish move into range, the heron will suddenly extend its neck and snatch it in its long sharp bill.

Whitefaced Ducks gather in their thousands at freshwater vleis and pans, mostly in the far northern and eastern reaches of southern Africa. They are also known as Whitefaced Whistling Ducks because of their high-pitched, whistling call.

THE WHISTLING SUITOR

Gaggling and posturing as they spill from mossy banks into dark still water, ducks and geese are synonymous with any large inland body of water.

Curiously, the male ducks of the southern hemisphere lack the range of colour of the males in the northern regions of the world. There, brilliantly hued plumage is part of the males' breeding garb for much of the year.

Nevertheless, even though they are less flamboyantly coloured, southern African ducks may bear distinctive markings and patterns, like the Whitefaced Duck with its neatly framed face and impeccably decorated body.

Since there is very little or no difference in appearance between the sexes, their breeding rituals rely heavily on creative vocalization, from raucous honking to gentle fluting. The Whitefaced Duck expresses itself with sweet whistling.

A Whitefaced Duck, or nonnetjie-eend (little nun) as it is called in Afrikaans, rafts placidly across the water. It dabbles and dives for food, constantly calling and interacting with other ducks that float alongside or congregate on the banks in small family groups.

The Goliath Heron is the largest heron in the world and attains a height of as much as 1,5 m. For its size, it is somewhat shy, though the young are quite aggressive in the nest and will lunge and clap their beaks if approached too closely.

Herons are among birds that have specialized feathers called powder down, which never moult but fray from the tip and continually grow from the base. The tips fray into a fine powder which the birds use to remove slime and oil from their feathers.

The broad wings of the Jackal Buzzard allow this resident of hilly country to hover almost motionless, with barely a flap of its wings, on the air currents over the crest of a hill. Poised to strike, it extends its formidable talons before swooping on small mammals, birds or reptiles.

Winged wonders of the air

Since time immemorial we have gazed skywards and marvelled at birds for their ability to swoop and soar, to hover, to dart about the sky, twisting and turning in brilliant aerobatic displays.

The Bearded Vulture can reach speeds as high as 130 km/h as it sweeps over its rugged habitat, while the trophy for the fastest bird must go to the Peregrine Falcon, which swoops into the attack at a speed of 350 km/h.

Then, there are some birds, such as the Jackal Buzzard, which can hang motionless, barely moving their wings, as they ride the updraught off a cliff or a hill.

But it is not only the larger species that are so accomplished, for some of the best flyers are also among the smallest. Some species of swifts, for instance, feed and sleep in the air and land only to breed or when ill. Such birds spend literally months in the air.

Birds also cover great distances, but the most amazing distance record is that set by a Common Tern. It flew 200 km a day for 18 weeks, covering 25 000 km in a flight from Finland, where it had been ringed, to Victoria, Australia.

Bearded Vultures will fly to a height of 40 m to drop bone material and smash it on the ground before consuming the fragments.

Awesome in the air, Bearded Vultures are superb and graceful flyers, riding the currents on wings spanning almost 3 m. They are strangely timid, despite their impressive dimensions, and are easily driven away from a carcass by other scavengers.

Hartlaub's Gulls often forage on the ground for food, but they have the agility to catch flying insects circling street lights at night.

RIDERS ON THE WIND

Many species, including sea birds and raptors such as the Bearded Vulture, ride air currents with barely a movement of their wings. The albatross, one of the most renowned gliders, tacks over the ocean, rapidly gliding downwind then turning into the slower-moving air near the surface of the sea and using it to gain height.

As speed decreases, it turns yet again, and glides down towards the surface, gaining speed in preparation for the next turn into the wind. These birds can stay aloft with little effort and cover long distances by using this method of flight.

Pelicans, however, use thermals to soar lazily near lakes and rivers. They gain height slowly on these rising columns of air before gliding down to skim over the placid waters. In common with other thermal soarers, their wings are broad and have wide slotted tips that help create a large surface area against which rising air currents can push.

Whitenecked Ravens and Peregrine Falcons are among the species that are slope soarers. They ride standing air waves, created when air is forced to rise over hills and cliffs. This technique allows these birds to remain in the same spot while scanning the surrounding area for food sources.

In addition to slope soaring, Whitenecked Ravens use thermals as well; they are often seen accompanying other scavengers such as vultures, as they inscribe great circles in the air, watching and waiting for prey.

Rising on wings that appear anything but preened to perfection, a Common Tern takes off from water. Once in full flight, however, it dips and swoops like a swallow, but usually hovers for a moment or two before plunging into the water after its prey.

Most birds, such as this gull, can take off in still air. Some of the larger gliding species, such as albatrosses, however, cannot take off at all unless a wind is blowing.

Comically ungainly on the ground, the Eastern White Pelican is a graceful performer in the air, soaring on wings that can span as much as 3 m. On the downstroke, the outer primary flight feathers flex and flare out, creating slots through which air can pass, reducing drag.

THE SWIFT AND SILENT HUNTERS

The elegant grace of a Whitebacked Vulture approaching a landing next to a carcass is matched by the power and prowess of an owl making its swift and silent attack on a hapless rodent.

High in the sky, the great bird rides a thermal in lazy circles. Then, in the distance, other vultures begin to descend. The Whitebacked Vulture instantly notices them doing so. It gracefully turns away from the thermal, losing height as it glides down towards the others in the distance, quickly closing on them at more than 60 km/h. As it nears the others, its speed increases until it is diving at almost 120 km/h. Then it slows as the ground rises to meet it.

Its legs are lowered for the landing and the wings begin to flare, acting like huge brakes.

At that moment, inboard of each wing tip, a small alula or 'bastard' wing flips open, smoothing the air flow over the wing, and the wing tip flight feathers splay out even more, flexing and providing the necessary lift at low speed.

The taloned feet touch the ground and the legs bend as they absorb the shock of landing. A short run ends it and, without a pause, the bird trots towards the carcass, wings outspread and head out-thrust.

In the dark of night, a Spotted Eagle Owl perches unseen on a branch. Nearby, a mouse forages busily through the grass. The bird turns towards the tiny sound and launches itself on silent wings.

Every sound the small mammal makes is clearly audible to the owl. It adjusts its flight, tracking its prey to the millimetre. In moments the hunt is over: the mouse is snatched in razor-sharp talons. Mercifully for the small rodent, death is instantaneous.

A Whitebacked Vulture about to land. Inboard of the splayed flight feathers, small 'bastard' wings smooth the air flow over the wing.

Lesser Kestrels feed on a range of aerial and terrestrial animals including scorpions, lizards and grasshoppers. They are agile flyers, usually hunting by flying low over the ground, abruptly turning into the wind to hover, and then swooping down. They also take prey in the air.

Insects, small mammals and birds make up the diet of the Spotted Eagle Owl. It catches its prey in powerful talons, and hunts at night, using its excellent auditory and visual senses to locate its prey. Flight is almost silent, allowing it to hear the sounds made by potential prey.

Wanderers feeding where the land meets the sea

The coastline of southern Africa stretches for over 5 000 km, its shape and mood dictated by the constant collision of water and landmass over millions of years. This is a shoreline of extreme contrasts, from the rugged headlands that stoically resist the angry clash of the Atlantic and Indian oceans off the southern tip of the African continent, to the calm stretches of beach where thick strands of blackened kelp lie strewn like unspooled film across the white sands.

About 20 local bird species breed along these shores, their numbers swelling with the arrival of scores of migrant visitors, some hailing from as far north as the Arctic Circle. The Sanderling is one such visitor, commonly seen in small flocks on sandy beaches, running along the water's edge like a clockwork toy, or picking through clumps of seaweed for tiny crustaceans and larvae.

Albatrosses, petrels and shearwaters circle the skies far out to sea, drawn from their breeding grounds on the Southern Ocean islands to the generous larder of the Benguela Current that sweeps along the west coast. Rarely seen from the shore, they circle and swoop around ships and fishing trawlers – the size and energy of their flocks indicating the abundance of fish, squid or crustaceans in the seas below them. Lagoons and estuaries, with their muddy banks and silt deposits, attract waders like the Eurasian Curlew, which uses its long decurved bill to probe deeply into the mud for prawns and marine worms.

Local marine birds include the Cape Cormorant, Cape Gannet and Jackass Penguin, each breeding in large colonies on offshore islands. The Jackass Penguin, loved for its Chaplinesque gait, is a delight to watch as it emerges at dawn from its nest under the bushes, between the enormous granite rocks at The Boulders on the Cape Peninsula, and sways unevenly onto the beach towards the gleaming water. It seems to be just waking up as it stands for a while at the water's edge, allowing the ripples to splash over its black webbed feet, before belly-flopping forward into the waves. As the sea closes over it, Africa's own penguin is now truly in its element. All at once swift, supple and graceful, perfectly in tune with the movement of the water, it sets off on a fishing trip that may take it about 10 km from the shore. The day is spent feeding on anchovies, sardines and squid. At dusk it returns, replete, to relieve its mate at their nest.

The shore offers a wealth of feeding opportunities to birds – on the rocks, in rock pools, in the sand or in the sea. An African Black Oystercatcher, red-eyed, with orange bill sharply contrasted against its sooty plumage, forages slowly along a rock-strewn shore on the west coast. It looks for mussels that are themselves feeding, with valves gaping. The bird quickly stabs its bill between the valves to cut the strong

MARINE

A group of Jackass Penguins emerges from the waves in the waning light of dusk as it returns from a day's fishing off the coast.

The Curlew Sandpiper breeds in the extreme northern part of Siberia and migrates in huge billowing flocks to enjoy the summers of the Southern Hemisphere. Foraging around open stretches of water, it uses its long beak to probe mud or sand for molluscs, worms and larvae.

muscle that holds them together. Then it removes the flesh from the valves, leaving them attached to the rock.

If the valves come away as it pulls on the flesh, however, the bird wedges the entire animal in a crack and chips a hole through a valve to reach the flesh.

With so much salt water being swallowed with their food, some marine birds would die of dehydration were it not for their remarkable nasal gland, which is specifically adapted to secrete the excess salt. Intensely salty droplets form on the sides of the nostrils or bill as they are secreted by the gland, and are shaken loose with a toss of the head.

There is a harmony and secret rhythm where the land meets the sea. The ebb and flow of the tide, as regular as breathing, reflect the phases of the moon while the arrival and departure of migratory birds mark the changing seasons. The same storms and high seas that endanger even the biggest ships, also churn up currents that carry a treasure trove of nourishment. There is an intricate and impeccable order built on strange alliances and unexpected relationships – enigmatic and reassuring.

A small silent flock of Bartailed Godwits rests along the water's edge. When feeding, they remain singularly focused as they push their slightly upcurved bills into the sand, searching for tiny marine creatures. In flight they often form a wavy line moving thinly across the water.

Cape Cormorants breed in dense colonies on rocky islands or guano platforms. The evenly spaced nests are substantial bowls of seaweed and plant debris strengthened with excreta.

The Whitebreasted Cormorant is unique in that it is the only southern African cormorant that frequents both marine and freshwater habitats. It fishes alone, its bill slicing easily and quickly through the water as it pursues its prey.

A cormorant's plumage is less water-repellent than that of other water birds – a surprising deficiency for an underwater fisher.
After a bout of swimming, the cormorant stands on dry land, wings outstretched, to dry i's waterlogged feathers in the sun.

A nesting Bank Cormorant throws up its wings in an enthusiastic gesture of welcome for its returning mate. A noticeable decline in the numbers of breeding pairs may be linked to a decrease in the abundance of rock lobster, particularly favoured by this sea bird.

FISHING FROM THE SKY

A flock of Cape Cormorants moves across the horizon, a dark undulating skein that, as though caught in a high wind, begins to unravel and spread out as it gets closer.

Drawn by the presence of a surface-shoaling mass of pilchards, the flock alights and the birds begin diving again and again for fish. Soon the birds at the rear of the shoal fly to the front of it for more fish, and as they leapfrog over the rest of the flock, it seems to roll over the surface of the sea.

They are the only native cormorant to follow shoals of fish in this way. While underwater, they hold their wings tightly to their body and propel themselves after the fleeing fish by paddling their webbed feet. This is the most numerous of the five cormorant species in southern Africa and it breeds in enormous colonies along the west coast.

The Bank Cormorant prefers to forage alone among kelp beds inshore, diving to depths of up to 28 m as it hunts for fish and crayfish.

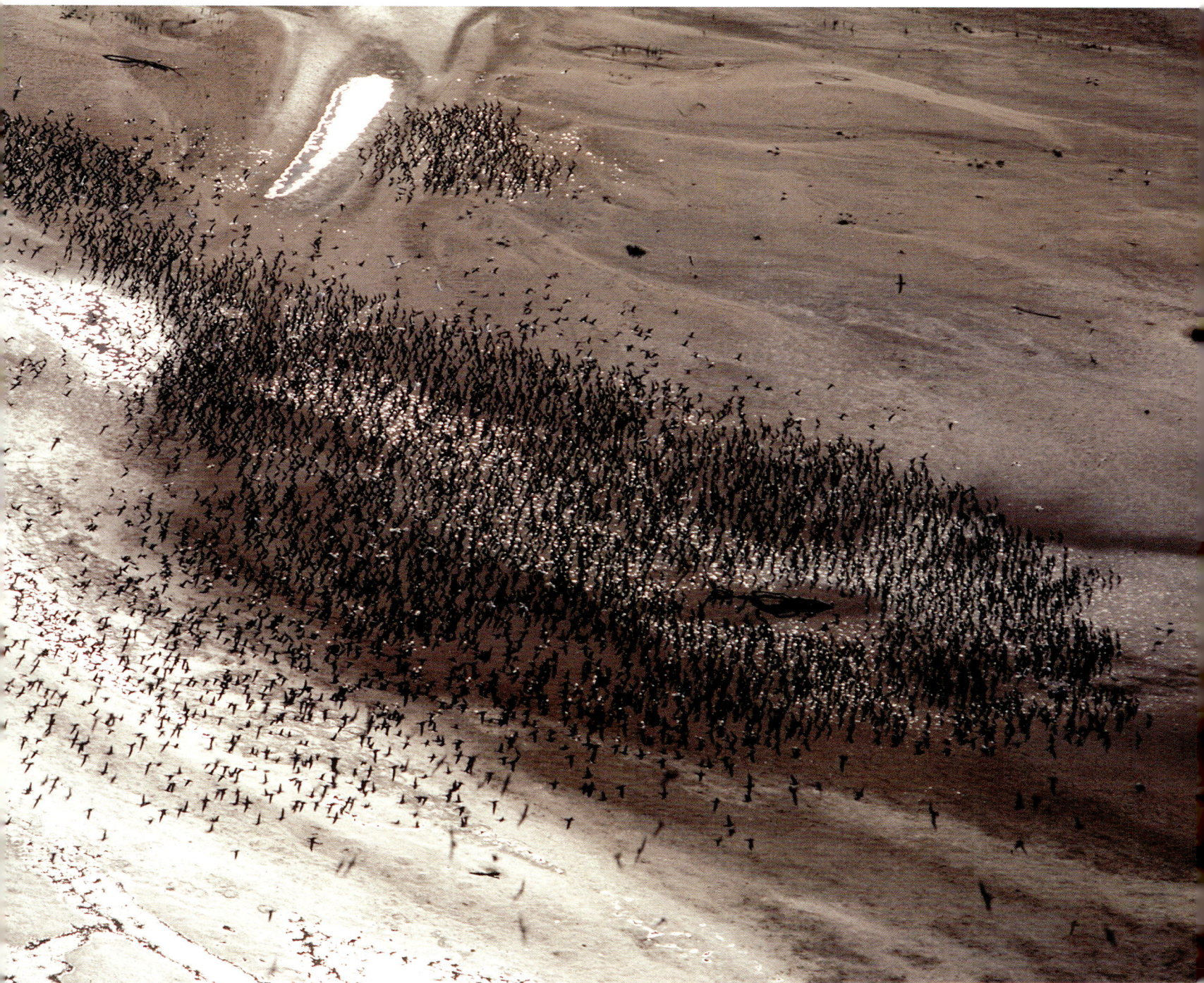

A mass of Cape Cormorants fills the skies over the Namib Desert coastline. They are drawn to this area in their thousands as their breeding season coincides with the strong winds that cause the surface water to move offshore and nutrient-rich water to well up in its place.

The African Black Oystercatcher is unmistakable, with its red eyes and flaming orange beak. Endemic to southern Africa, this is a typical shore bird, breeding on islands, rocky coasts and sandy beaches where strands of blackened kelp help to conceal it when it's nesting.

Elegantly balanced, feathers ruffling in the sea breeze, a Greyheaded Gull delicately preens itself. A highly nomadic scavenger with a strong survival instinct, this is the only resident gull in Africa to have adapted to a freshwater environment. It ranges widely over the subcontinent.

Cape Gannets hunt from the air, scanning the sea for moving shadows beneath the surface. When a bird spots a fish, it plummets into the water in an exquisite dive, entering the sea at an oblique angle and streamlining itself by holding its wings tightly against its body.

ISLANDS OF FEATHERS AND POINTING BEAKS

An island colony of Cape Gannets is an amazing spectacle; a constant movement of sleek, whitefeathered bodies with orangetinted heads that stretch and bow, and point sharp grey beaks skywards like so many drawn swords.

The ability to communicate distinctly by gesture or display is particularly important in a dense colony. The peculiar 'sky-pointing' is a way of indicating an intention to take off. This gesture is almost one of appeasement, the bird appearing to 'apologise' for disturbing its neighbours as it moves slowly, wings spread, towards the edge of the community from where it will be able to take to the air.

A misunderstood intention can provoke a vicious fight that will disrupt the community and disturb the equilibrium that holds the multitude in its state of relative harmony. And yet, this frenetic mass of adults and chicks manages in the midst of courting, incubation and irritable squabbling to avoid injuring one another.

There is something to be learned in the way a returning parent finds its nest among the many thousands of others and maintains its own household in such crowded conditions.

The elegant orange tint on this Cape Gannet's head will fade after the breeding season. Gannets have especially strong skulls to withstand the impact as they plunge into the water. They also have subcutaneous air sacs in the neck and breast to absorb the shock of the impact.

A Cape Gannet indicates its intention to take off by 'sky-pointing'. The bold stripe down the throat accentuates the display.

A Cape Gannet takes time out to preen itself. Mutual preening, referred to as allopreening, between a gannet and its mate is an important way of strengthening their bond as a pair.

Highly sociable and intensely active, Cape Gannets have a rich repertoire of gestures and behaviour that helps to maintain some order in their crowded community. They breed only in southern Africa, mostly off the west coast.

A Jackass Penguin strides with uncommon stateliness into the sea. Its name is derived from its loud braying call, but there are those who would like to restore some dignity to the bird by distinguishing it rather as the African or Blackfooted Penguin.

They prefer to nest in burrows dug in guano deposits, but the depletion of these has led to Jackass Penguins making their nests above ground. They place rocks on the edge of the nest.

Penguins spend a large part of their lives in the sea. During breeding, each parent takes a turn at the nest while the other takes full advantage of its time off to hunt, swim or simply wallow in the water before returning to shore.

FLIGHTLESS BIRDS THAT SWIM LIKE FISH

To see a Jackass Penguin transformed from a bumbling caricature, swaying on squat legs with scaly flippers hanging pointlessly at its sides, to an agile, swiftly moving swimmer is a strangely exhilarating experience. It is a metamorphosis that challenges the easy assumptions we make about the way a creature looks or moves. More comfortable in the water than out, it lives entirely off the bounty of the sea, eating about 540 g of fish a day.

On some islands the penguin populations are going up and on others they are declining. The precise reasons for these changes are not fully understood, but they are probably linked to the food supply.

Surprisingly, in 1985 they began to colonize The Boulders, a sheltered cove on the False Bay shore. It is close to residential areas, but even though its proximity to humans has increased the penguins' vulnerability, their numbers have steadily grown and this particular colony has become a major tourist attraction.

Penguins often toboggan into the water. Here their bellies are discoloured by algae which was rubbed into their breast feathers as they slid down to the water. They use their feet for propulsion if the slope is not steep enough to let gravity do the work.

When moulting, which peaks between November and January, Jackass Penguins are land-bound for approximately 3 weeks. During this time they may lose almost half of their body weight.

Fabulous, functional feathers – multicoloured, multipurpose

Feathers really set birds apart from any other living organism. They facilitate flight, they shape and insulate, disguise and protect, and they flash and gleam like jewellery.

They are made of keratin (as are our hair and nails) and their construction imparts strength, flexibility and an unmatched ability to withstand damage. The central rib is called the shaft or rachis and supports the barbs – thin hair-like arms branching off the shaft. These barbs in turn are linked by barbules. Those facing towards the base of the feather are plain, whereas those facing away from it have small hooklets, called barbicels. These hook onto the plain barbules and hold the barbs together.

This fine lattice presents the appearance of a solid surface. But the truth is very different. If a feather's barbs are separated, by the blow of another bird's beak, for instance, they can be quickly preened back into place so that the barbules again lock together and hold the barbs in place.

The body feathers of the Cape Gannet insulate and streamline the body for flight and for plunging below the surface of the sea in pursuit of shoaling fish such as pilchards. Body feathers are softer and shorter than flight feathers, shape the body and protect the bird in cold weather.

The speckled primary feathers of the Helmeted Guineafowl camouflage the bird in the undergrowth by breaking up its shape and solid colour. Another speckled species, the Freckled Nightjar, is so well camouflaged that it can safely nest on boulders and remain unnoticed.

Perhaps the most dazzling feathers are those of the peacock, which spreads its tail feathers in a truly magnificent display of shimmering colour.

Just as fascinating, however, are the breast feathers of the Namaqua Sandgrouse. They have split and teased barbs, providing a loose matlike material that absorbs water. The male soaks these feathers at a water hole or river, and then returns to its young, which drink from its plumage.

The metallic areas on the wing feathers of the Greenspotted Dove provide vivid splashes of colour. The green iridescence is caused when different layers of melanin – a pigment which produces blacks, browns and yellows – interfere with light rays.

The bright red, green and blue of the Rosyfaced Lovebirds' primary feathers make this bird attractively distinctive. The pattern and regularity of the primary feathers contrast with the softer body feathers. These have downlike barbs near the bases, which help to insulate the bird.

The egg — nature's perfect varicoloured package

The khaki colour, dark speckling and scrolling of African Black Oystercatcher eggs provide excellent camouflage, making them resemble pebbles and breaking up their shape so that they merge with the background of this stony shell-strewn beach.

Eggs come in a range of colours and a variety of shapes and sizes. They may be white, speckled or spotted, or greenish-blue like the Cape Weaver's. Some species' eggs may vary – the Swift Tern's can be cream, buff, pale pink, turquoise or whitish, though all are streaked with brown and deep mauve.

Louries lay round eggs, swifts lay oval ones, the egg of the smallest species of hummingbird weighs as little as 0,2 g and that of an Ostrich as much as 1,6 kg, 8 000 times heavier, yet both perform exactly the same functions perfectly.

African Black Oystercatchers usually lay two eggs. The nest is a shallow scrape in the sand near blackened kelp or among stones where the eggs and the birds are less noticeable. If disturbed they leave the nest and draw the intruder away with loud calls and conspicuous displays.

A MULTIPURPOSE MASTERPIECE

An egg is a self-contained package that provides the ideal environment for the developing embryo and just about everything it will need – apart from warmth. It is a masterpiece of natural engineering, which looks deceptively simple but is actually quite complex.

The calcium carbonate shell protects the embryo from predators and, to some extent, from excessive heat. It is also perforated with thousands of tiny pores which allow the diffusion of air into the egg and carbon dioxide out of it.

While it is being incubated, the egg loses water and becomes lighter – which is why the test for a fresh egg is to place it in water. If fresh, it sinks; if well incubated, it floats.

A few days before they hatch, chicks begin to produce a sharp 'clicking' sound which helps to synchronize hatching of the clutch. Then, just before hatching, they use their chalky egg tooth on the tip of their bill to make a ring of

African Skimmer nestlings and eggs are coloured to blend in with the sand. In hot weather the parents soak their belly feathers in order to wet the eggs and the nestlings to keep them cool. They may also partly bury the eggs and the nestlings for the same purpose.

holes in the blunt end of the egg. Straightening their body with a heave, they force this caplike piece of shell off the egg and struggle out of it. The egg tooth is usually reabsorbed or lost within a few days of hatching.

The length of time an egg has to be incubated varies from species to species. For instance, the Cape White-eye's eggs can begin hatching as little as 11 days after being laid, while the Bateleur nestling will hatch after about 55 days.

Blacknecked Grebe eggs are white when newly hatched but are soon stained brown by the wet nesting material. These birds may cover their eggs with this material when they are disturbed and have to leave the nest. Dabchicks and Great Crested Grebes almost always do so.

Index

Glossary

ALIEN – refers to a species that has been introduced from another part of the world and which is not indigenous to the area under discussion.

ALULA – a small feathered structure (also known as a bastard wing) on the leading edge of the wing which smooths the airflow over the wing.

ALTRICIAL – refers to a young bird that stays in the nest until able to fly and is totally dependent on its parents until then.

AQUATIC – refers to a species that lives in close association with water

BROOD PARASITISM – the use of a host species to raise the young of another species (the parasite). Well-known examples include cuckoos, honeyguides and whydahs.

CAINISM – the process whereby the first-hatched nestling kills any younger sibling. The process is named after Cain, first son of Adam and Eve, who killed his younger brother Abel. Cainism occurs among eagles, for example.

CARRION – the remains of a dead animal.

CERE – the area of bare skin (not to be confused with a wattle) at the base of the upper mandible which also surrounds the nostrils.

COLONIAL – refers to the manner in which the individuals of a species live in close proximity. This usually occurs during the breeding season when a number of individuals of a particular species build their nests close together, so creating a colony.

COVERTS – the smaller feathers on the tail and wings, that cover the bases of the flight feathers.

CREPUSCULAR – active at dawn and/or dusk.

CROP – the portion of a bird's oesophagus which is used to store or partly digest food before it is passed into the gizzard. After feeding, a crop of a vulture, for instance, bulges prominently.

DECURVED – refers to a bill that has a downward curve.

DISRUPTIVE COLORATION – the arrangement of spots, bars and other elements of a pattern of coloration that breaks up the outline of the bird and improves its camouflage.

DIURNAL – active during the day.

EGG TOOTH – a chalky point on the end of a hatchling's beak which it uses to chip its way out of the egg. The egg tooth is lost soon after the chick has hatched.

ENDEMIC – native to, and restricted to, a specified geographical region.

EXOTIC – see ALIEN.

FULVOUS – refers to plumage with a tawny or reddish-yellow colour.

GAPE – the angle of the junction between the upper and lower parts of the bill at its base. This term also refers to the wide opening of the beak itself.

GREGARIOUS – refers to the habit of some species that live together in large groups or flocks.

HABITAT – the particular environment in which a species lives.

INDIGENOUS – refers to a species that is native to a particular habitat or area.

IMMATURE – refers to a bird that has moulted out of its first juvenile plumage but not yet grown its full adult coloration.

JUVENILE – the stage at which a young bird attains its first full-feathered plumage.

MONTANE – relating to mountains.

NESTLING – a term for ALTRICIAL young

NIDICOLOUS – see ALTRICIAL.

NIDIFUGOUS – see PRECOCIAL.

NOCTURNAL – active during the hours of darkness.

OSSUARY – flat platform of rock on which Bearded Vultures drop long bones to break them in order to get at the marrow.

PELAGIC – refers to birds that spend most of their lives over the ocean and return to land only to breed.

PRECOCIAL – refers to a young bird that is able to leave the nest soon after hatching. Fully precocial young feed themselves exclusively; sub-precocial are fed at least in part by their parents.

PRIMARIES – the outer flight feathers of a bird's wing. They are attached to the bones of the hand.

RAPTORS – birds of prey of the order Falconiformes, such as buzzards, eagles, falcons and hawks but excluding owls (which belong to the order Strigiformes).

RANGE – the geographical region or regions over which a species is distributed.

RECURVED – refers to a bill that has an upward curve.

RESIDENT – refers to a species that remains in the same region through the year.

RUFOUS – refers to plumage with a reddish-brown colour.

SECONDARIES – the flight feathers between the primaries and the bird's body which are attached to the ulna.

TERRESTRIAL – living on land.

TERRITORY – the specific area a bird establishes, usually for breeding, and then defends against intruders, mainly members of the same species. Territory defence may be accomplished by means of advertising (through calls, for example), display from a vantage point or aggression.

VAGRANT – a species that is a rare and accidental visitor to the region under discussion.

WATTLE – a bare, fleshy area of skin (often it is a rich colour and sometimes pendulous) on the head of a bird. Often the wattle is around the eye, on the throat or at the junction of the upper and lower parts of the bill.

Photographic credits

Photographic credits for each page read from top to bottom, using the top of the picture as the reference point.

Abbreviations:
ABPL – Anthony Bannister Photo Library;
FP – Focal Point;
NPB – Natal Parks Board;
PA – Photo Access.

All maps are the copyright of The Reader's Digest Association South Africa (Pty) Limited

Front cover JJ Brooks/PA
Back cover Colin Paterson-Jones

1 Terry Carew/PA
2 Daryl Balfour/ABPL
4 Peter Pickford/FP
5 Alan Wilson/PA
6 Alan Wilson/PA
8 Peter Craig-Cooper
10 Colin Paterson-Jones
12 Colin Paterson-Jones; Peter & Beverly Pickford/FP
13 HPH Photography/PA
14 Nigel J Dennis
15 Roger de la Harpe/NPB
16 Colin Paterson-Jones
17 Colin Paterson-Jones
18 Nico Myburgh
19 Nigel J Dennis/ABPL
20 Nigel J Dennis
21 Beverly Joubert/ABPL; Nigel J Dennis
22 Nigel J Dennis/ABPL; Ivor Migdoll
23 Nigel J Dennis/ABPL
24 Lex Hes
26 Warwick Tarboton/ABPL
27 Nigel J Dennis; Nigel J Dennis/ABPL
28 Nigel J Dennis/ABPL
29 Lanz von Hörsten
30 Peter Craig-Cooper
31 Nico Myburgh
32 Colin Paterson-Jones
33 Roger de la Harpe
34 Nico Myburgh
35 Nigel J Dennis
36 Lorna Stanton/ABPL
37 Lex Hes
38 Warwick Tarboton/ABPL
39 JJ Brooks/PA
40 Peter Steyn/PA
41 Roger de la Harpe
42 P Chadwick
43 Roger de la Harpe/ABPL
44 Peter Pickford/FP
45 Colin Paterson-Jones
46 JJ Brooks/PA
47 J & B Photographers/PA
48 Hein von Hörsten
49 Lanz von Hörsten
50 Roger de la Harpe/NPB; Nico Myburgh
51 Anthony Bannister/ABPL
52 Hein von Hörsten

53 Hein von Hörsten
54 David Steele/PA
56 Rob Ponte/ABPL
57 Lex Hes
58 Roger de la Harpe
59 Nigel J Dennis
60 Nigel J Dennis/ABPL
61 Johan Beyers
62 Lex Hes
63 Lex Hes
64 Nigel J Dennis
65 Nigel J Dennis
66 Roger de la Harpe
67 Roger de la Harpe
68 Ivor Migdoll
69 Lisa Trocchi/ABPL
70 Roger de la Harpe/ABPL
71 Roger de la Harpe
72 Lorna Stanton/ABPL
73 Peter Pickford/FP
74 Alan Wilson/PA
75 Anthony Bannister/ABPL
76 Nico Myburgh
77 Roger de la Harpe
78 Both JJ Brooks/PA
79 Lex Hes
80 Lex Hes
81 Ivor Migdoll; Peter Steyn/PA
82 Lex Hes; Lanz von Hörsten
83 Johan van Jaarsveld/ABPL
84 Lanz von Hörsten
86 Martin Harvey/ABPL
87 Warwick Tarboton/ABPL
88 HPH Photography/PA
89 Warwick Tarboton/ABPL
90 Clem Haagner/ABPL
91 Roger de la Harpe/ABPL
92 Hein von Hörsten
93 Peter Craig-Cooper
94 Lanz von Hörsten
95 Roger de la Harpe/ABPL
96 Johan van Jaarsveld/ABPL
97 Nigel J Dennis
98 Nigel J Dennis
99 Lex Hes
100 Terry Carew/PA
101 HPH Photography/PA
102 Clem Haagner/ABPL
103 Alan Weaving/PA
104 Roger de la Harpe; Lex Hes
105 Peter Craig-Cooper
106 Hein von Hörsten/ABPL
107 Peter Craig-Cooper
108 Roger de la Harpe
109 Lex Hes
110 Warwick Tarboton/ABPL
111 Peter Craig-Cooper
112 Peter Lillie/ABPL
113 Alan Wilson/PA
114 Nigel J Dennis
115 Lex Hes
116 Anthony Bannister/ABPL
117 GPL du Plessis/PA
118 HPH Photography/PA
119 Nigel J Dennis
120 Ivor Migdoll
121 Peter Craig-Cooper
122 Lex Hes
123 Lex Hes
124 Beverly Joubert/ABPL
125 Nigel J Dennis/ABPL

126 Daryl Balfour/ABPL
127 Helmut Niebuhr/ABPL
128 Lanz von Hörsten
129 Hein von Hörsten
130 Warwick Tarboton/ABPL
131 JJ Brooks/PA
132 Lex Hes
134 Nigel J Dennis/ABPL; Thomas Dressler/ABPL
135 Lex Hes
136 Peter Craig-Cooper
137 Nigel J Dennis/ABPL
138 GPL du Plessis/PA
139 Nigel J Dennis
140 Lorna Stanton/ABPL
141 Colin Paterson-Jones; Gavin Thomson/ABPL
142 Daryl Balfour/ABPL
143 Joan Ryder/ABPL
144 Lex Hes
145 M Philip Kahl/ABPL
146 Colin Paterson-Jones
147 Nigel J Dennis
148 Alan Wilson/PA
149 Peter Lillie/ABPL; HPH Photography/PA
150 GPL du Plessis/PA
151 Johan van Jaarsveld/ABPL
152 Lex Hes; Nigel J Dennis
153 Gerald Hinde/ABPL
154 Nigel J Dennis
155 Alan Wilson/PA
156 Nico Myburgh
157 Johan van Jaarsveld/ABPL
158 Nigel J Dennis
159 Nigel J Dennis
160 Both Ivor Migdoll
161 Ivor Migdoll
162 Nigel J Dennis
163 Nigel J Dennis/ABPL
164 Lex Hes
166 Anthony Bannister/ABPL
167 Brendan Ryan/ABPL
168 David Steele/PA; Daryl Balfour/ABPL
169 Terry Carew/ABPL
170 HPH Photography/PA; Nigel J Dennis
171 Peter Craig-Cooper
172 HPH Photography/PA
173 John Paisley/PA
174 HPH Photography/PA
175 Alan Wilson/PA; Colin Paterson-Jones
176 Peter Pickford/FP
177 JJ Brooks/PA
178 Nigel J Dennis
179 Anthony Bannister/ABPL; Peter Pickford/FP
180 Lex Hes; Aron Frankental/ABPL
181 Terry Carew/PA
182 Nigel J Dennis
183 Anthony Bannister/ABPL; Lex Hes
184 Both Nigel J Dennis
185 Alan Wilson/PA
186 Peter & Beverly Pickford/FP
188 HPH Photography/PA
189 Nigel J Dennis/ABPL
190 Peter Craig-Cooper

191 Nigel J Dennis
192 Aron Frankental/ABPL
193 Ron Crous/ABPL
194 Peter Craig-Cooper
195 HPH Photography/PA
196 Tim Liversedge/ABPL; Johan Beyers
197 Nigel J Dennis/ABPL
198 Alan Wilson/PA
199 Nigel J Dennis/ABPL
200 Alan Wilson/PA
201 Nigel J Dennis; Nigel J Dennis/ABPL
202 Peter Craig-Cooper
203 Nigel J Dennis/ABPL
204 Ivor Migdoll
205 Ivor Migdoll
206 Alan Wilson/PA
207 Alan Wilson/PA
208 Daryl Balfour/ABPL
209 Roger de la Harpe
210 Nigel J Dennis
211 Nigel J Dennis
212 Ivor Migdoll
213 Nigel J Dennis
214 Roger de la Harpe/NPB; Nigel J Dennis/ABPL
215 Alan Wilson/PA
216 Thomas Dressler/ABPL
217 Alan Wilson/PA
218 Roger de la Harpe
219 Roger de la Harpe
220 Alan Wilson/PA
221 Alan Wilson/PA
222 Nigel J Dennis
223 Nigel J Dennis/ABPL; Roger de la Harpe
224 Lex Hes; Alan Wilson/PA
225 Ivor Migdoll; Nigel J Dennis
226 Nigel J Dennis; Nico Myburgh
227 Nico Myburgh
228 Peter Pickford/FP
230 Nigel J Dennis
231 Clem Haagner/ABPL
232 David Steele/PA; Alan Wilson/PA
233 Lorna Stanton/ABPL
234 Anthony Bannister/ABPL
235 Anthony Bannister/ABPL
236 Lex Hes
237 Ivor Migdoll
238 Lanz von Hörsten
239 Lex Hes
240 Lex Hes
241 Hein von Hörsten; Pat de la Harpe/PA
242 Nigel J Dennis
243 Both Peter Pickford/FP
244 Anthony Bannister/ABPL
245 Anthony Bannister/ABPL
246 Shaen Adey/ABPL
247 M Philip Kahl/ABPL
248 Lex Hes
249 Anthony Bannister/ABPL
250 Lex Hes
251 Nico Myburgh
252 Anthony Bannister/ABPL
253 JJ Brooks/PA

Digital scanning and repro by Scan Shop, Cape Town. Printed by Tien Wah Press (Pte) Ltd, Singapore.